DIVIDEND MILLIONAIRE

By Matt Miller

HOW TO REACH A MILLION DOLLAR DIVIDEND PORTFOLIO

PLUS

- COMPLETE ANALYSIS ON TWENTY OF THE BEST DIVIDEND STOCKS TO BUY FOR 2014
- HOW TO STRATEGICALLY MANAGE YOUR PORTFOLIO WITH PROPER DIVERSIFICATION, ALLOCATION, AND TAX AVOIDANCE

Copyright © 2014 by Matt Miller

All rights reserved. No part of this publication may be reproduced, distributed, or transmitted in any form or by any means, including photocopying, recording, or other electronic or mechanical methods, without the prior written permission of the publisher, except in the case of brief quotations embodied in critical reviews and certain other noncommercial uses permitted by copyright law. For permission requests, write to the publisher, addressed "Attention: Permissions Coordinator," at the address below.

TFS Publishing P.O. Box 36081 Baltimore, MD 21286
www.thefinanceshow.com

This book is designed to provide accurate and authoritative information on the subject of investing. It is sold with the understanding that neither the Author nor the Publisher is engaged in rendering legal, accounting, or other professional services by publishing this book. As each individual situation is unique, questions relevant to investing and specific to the individual should be addressed to an appropriate professional to ensure that the situation has been evaluated carefully and appropriately. The Author and Publisher specifically disclaim any liability, loss, or risk that is incurred as a consequence, directly or indirectly, of the use and application of any of the contents of this work.

ISBN-13: 978-0692027820 (TFS Publishing)

ISBN-10: 0692027823

Printed in the United States of America

First Edition

This book is dedicated with love to my wife, Jennifer, and to my remarkable children, Luke and Ava, collectively my inspiration for all things in life.

Table of Contents

Preface	7
Chapter 1: Living Off Dividends	11
Chapter 2: Allocation & Diversification	21
Chapter 3: Phillip Morris International	31
Chapter 4: Realty Income Corporation	35
Chapter 5: The Southern Company	39
Chapter 6: McDonald's Corporation	43
Chapter 7: Kraft Food Corporation	47
Chapter 8: ConAgra Foods Corporation	51
Chapter 9: The Coca-Cola Corporation	53
Chapter 10: Pepsico, Inc.	57
Chapter 11: Potash Corp. of Saskatchewan	61
Chapter 12: Conoco Philips	65
Chapter 13: Altria Group, Inc.	67
Chapter 14: Kinder Morgan Partners, L.P.	71
Chapter 15: Enterprise Products Partners, L.P.	75
Chapter 16: Kinder Morgan, Inc.	77
Chapter 17: Kimberly Clark Corp	81
Chapter 18: Proctor & Gamble	85

Chapter 19: Johnson & Johnson	89
Chapter 20: The Clorox Company	93
Chapter 21: AT&T	95
Chapter 22: Verizon Communications, Inc.	97
Chapter 23: Taxes	99
Chapter 24: Inflation	105
Chapter 25: Reaching a Million	109
Acknowledgements	123
Appendix	124
References	126

Preface

When the Great Recession of 2008-2009 hit the stock market, many investors saw their retirement savings get cut in half or worse. Those same investors could not stand to lose anymore and sold their equity positions at steep losses. This barred them from participating in the market rally that began in March of 2009. They sat in fear and in cash, not willing to risk any more of their hard earned money. Who would blame them? It's human nature to protect what we have. If these same investors had invested in high quality dividend growth stocks, they wouldn't have seen their portfolio lose as much as the greater market (because of the low-beta nature of most dividend stocks - see Chapter 2). Their mindset would have also been different, because dividend growth investors don't mind seeing the price of their stock decline. A decline in a stock means that it's on sale, and its dividend yield is increasing as the stock is declining (as long as a company doesn't cut its dividend, the dividend yield always rises as the stock declines). Dividend growth investors will often add to their positions in down markets, enticed by ever-increasing dividend yields and lower stock prices.

Dividend Millionaire will show you how you can achieve a million dollar portfolio with the help of dividend growth investing and a long runway. This book is meant for the intermediate to advanced investor, not the beginner. There are plenty of books on the shelf for the beginning investor. This book is designed as the next level, offering practical stock picks and in-depth knowledge on many aspects of investing, and focusing on dividend growth investing. Dividend stocks aren't just for retirees and widowers; no, quite the opposite in fact. If you're young and start investing in dividend stocks at an early age (under 40), the effects of compounding will be tremendous to your portfolio. If you're older and use your current nest egg, dividend stocks can provide the money to live off of during your retirement.

Dividend Millionaire is divided into three different parts. The first part goes over living off of dividends, diversification, and allocation. Would you believe that going over a certain number of stocks in your portfolio is detrimental to growth? Did you know that the ideal position size for each stock in your portfolio is between 3.5 and 6 percent of the total portfolio? How is it possible to live off of those measly dividend payments? We'll go over all of that in part one.

The second part is an analysis of the twenty best dividend growth stocks you can buy for your portfolio for 2014 and beyond. Some books may give you an analysis and tell you that it's a good starting point for further research (not this book). I give twenty stock recommendations and tell you that these are the best dividend stocks you can buy today. Buy the stocks listed in this book if you're a dividend growth investor and want to be rewarded financially. An investor can go into "analysis paralysis", reviewing all of the information that is publicly available for many companies, without putting a buy order in for any stock. As an investor, you're probably the analytical type who likes to review a company's quantitative and qualitative information in order to make an informed decision. Looking for marginal data on a company may make you feel like you're smarter than the other guy, allowing you to feel safe with the stocks you picked. As investors, we tend to be overly confident in our ability to pick "winners". Then once we pick a company to invest in, we look for further evidence that our decision was correct. We then discount evidence that might be contrary to our decision. It may not be useful to analyze companies beyond a certain point; instead, after you purchase a stock, look forward to your next investment opportunity. If a stock is good enough to purchase, then you shouldn't necessarily keep analyzing it, once a year should suffice.

The third part goes into the effects of inflation, taxation, and finally reaching your million-dollar portfolio. Having these topics lumped together in the same section will make it easier to look at the effects of inflation and taxation on your money. Investing your money efficiently in tax-favored accounts and in companies that can withstand inflation will make achieving success much easier. You could shave ten years off of your goal just by making sure you're not overpaying for taxes and that your portfolio isn't eaten up by inflation.

The Emperor Has No Clothes

Today many investors are empowered by the internet, but there are also pitfalls to having information at your fingertips 24/7. If you want to invest in a certain company, you've probably researched the company on the internet. There are many sites dedicated to researching companies and giving recommendations on buying and selling. Most of these sites are either trying to sell subscription services or are simply making money from advertisements on their site. Stay away from the subscription sites. Most subscription sites can't be trusted to provide the investor with valuable information. Many times, these subscription sites run the same exact articles multiple times a year. Some sites will give you their investment picks for a small monthly fee. I'm afraid to say that most of these sites are a huge rip-off. Why would you pay someone to give you (usually bad) stock picks? This is something that you can do for yourself with little effort. The problem is that many investors think that there is some sort of secret to picking just the right stocks. Investment hucksters offer their "secret" investment picks at a price. Oftentimes, these hucksters will come up with unheard of companies that don't generate profit. You, as the investor, feel like you're getting your money's worth because you've never heard of this company before. It must be the next Facebook or Berkshire Hathaway. The problem is that it's not the next great technology company or insurance conglomerate. It's more likely to go to zero than to go up for any extended period of time.

The Investor and the Internet

When it comes to making decisions, some internet savvy investors will get information overload, and have a hard time making a decision at all. Some sites will tell you to buy a certain stock, others say sell. The amount of financial information listed on the web is tremendous. You may look at financial information and see that the P/E ratio for one stock is lower than another. So, you decide to buy the stock with the lower P/E ratio. After all, both companies are in the same industry and grow revenues and earnings at the same rate. You're brilliant! You just out-smarted the market by finding this lower P/E ratio on the web. You hold your newly purchased stock for a year and it underperforms the entire time. What went wrong? What you didn't see on the financials is that the company you purchased had higher earnings because of a one-time sale of an asset that had to be recorded as revenue under generally accepted accounting principles. This lowered the P/E ratio at the time you purchased it, but in the future the earnings drop and the P/E ratio goes up.

Reading books on investing is much more reliable than surfing the internet for investment information. The problem investors face is that investment information can quickly become obsolete. There are some great sources on the internet that you can rely on. Annual reports (or 10-Ks) that companies publish on their own websites are great. You can get insight into what direction management is taking the company. The numbers on the annual report don't lie. Companies have to use GAAP to file their reports; however, most companies will highlight the good information and try to hide the bad. Many companies report some form of pro forma earnings (non-GAAP) that they say represents the business more clearly. There may be some truth to that, but don't pay attention to these pro forma measurements.

Chapter 1

Living Off Dividends

It is possible, through astute investing, to live off of the dividend income your portfolio generates. Dividends often start as tiny quarterly payments to the owner of stock in a company. With careful consideration, when building a portfolio, investors can expect ever-increasing dividends that occur several times a month. There is a possibility that you can be paid more frequently by a dividend than by your paycheck. Your stream of income will increase through the years, with good dividend-paying companies doubling their dividends every seven years.

Although your dividends may double every seven years, it's important to consider inflation when thinking about living off of dividends. What if the price you pay for consumption goods doubles every seven years? Or, what if the rate of inflation is higher than that of dividend increases? Inflation is the biggest enemy of the dividend growth investor. It can destroy your returns if your portfolio is not set up correctly. Research on inflation and how to set up your portfolio to hedge against inflation is located in Chapter 24.

The first thing you should figure out is how much money you need each year in order to live. Let's figure that all of your debts are paid off. This needs to be the case if you plan on living off of dividend income. With that in mind, you still have to pay taxes, insurance, gas, grocery, utility, and other miscellaneous bills – it takes a lot of money to live, even when you become debt free! Figure this number out for yourself. Make sure to include property tax; that can be a big one depending on your location. For the below examples, we use $50,000 and $20,000 total annual expenses, respectively.

The next thing is to figure out what percentage return you're getting on your dividends each year. If your portfolio returns 3.7 percent in dividends each, you would need $1,351,351 to generate $50,000 per year. For most beginning investors, this amount seems high. That's probably why a lot of dividend investors lose their patience and start chasing high-flying returns that are likely to blow up their portfolio. If your living expenses are only $20,000 per year, your portfolio doesn't need to be as big. A $500,000 portfolio would generate over $20,000 annually at a dividend rate of approximately 4.5 percent. One of the great things about being a dividend investor is that doing nothing will work to your advantage. Once you have a solid dividend portfolio, you simply have to wait for your dividends to grow each and every year.

Assume you've now invested in dividend paying stocks for 21 years. Your original rate in year one was 3.7 percent, but that has since grown. You've invested in companies that increase their dividends regularly and now have a yield on cost of 29.6 percent. That means that for every $1,000 you invested in year 1, you receive an annual dividend of $296 in year 21. Most investors will be purchasing additional shares throughout their accumulation phase, so this will place downward pressure on total yield on cost. For example, $1,000 invested in year 1 combined with $1000 in year 21 will produce a total yield on cost of 16.65 percent.

This amazing compounding effect makes it much easier to accumulate enough in dividend income to live off of. For simplification, let's assume that you can manage to save enough and accumulate a dividend portfolio valued at $500,000 by 2020. This is no easy feat, and depending on your current portfolio value, you may need to adjust the year or portfolio value. The chart below shows the dividends being paid out starting in year 2020 on a $500,000 portfolio and the expenses per year.

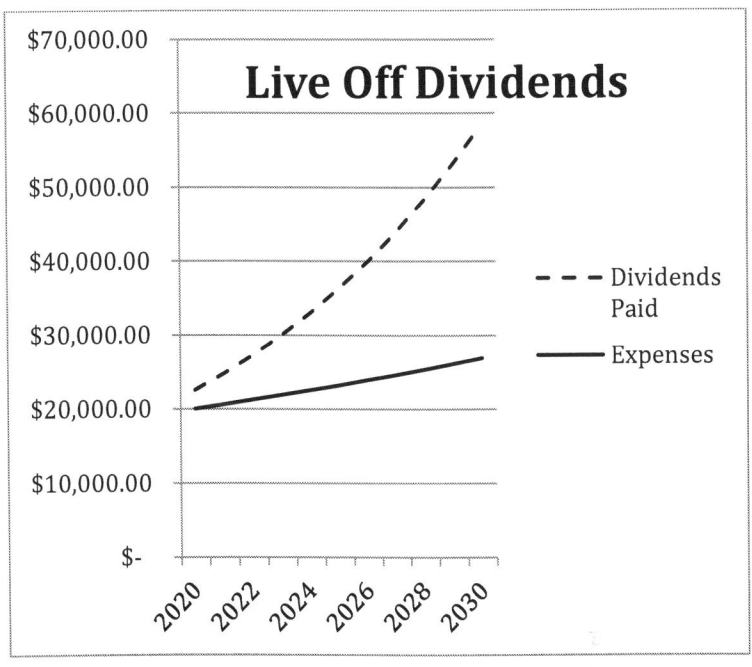

Here are the assumptions:

	Inputs Below
Principle	$500,000.00
Dividend Growth	10.00%
Current Yield	4.50%
Annual Expenses	$20,000
Increase in Annual Expenses	3.00%
Retirement Year	2020

Dividends paid out in year one of this scenario total $22,500, while expenses are listed at $20,000. We assume a 10 percent growth rate in dividend payments and a 3 percent growth rate in annual expenses. Notice how in year 1 the difference between the dividend payments and expense is $2,500. This means that this person/household can live off of their dividend payments alone. If it were negative, they would have to draw down on principle, get a job, or tap a credit card. At year 2030, dividends paid are $58,359 and expense are $26,878. Notice the difference is $31,481, much higher than the initial year's difference. This is the power of compounding dividend payments. You need a long stretch of time to see the effects of growth; this is no get rich quick way of investing.

A Tale of Two Outcomes

Now let's look at two different college graduates entering the workforce. These days, college graduates have a difficult time getting a college-level job quickly. Both of our graduates, against the odds, land a decent job after college each making about $40,000 plus benefits. Sarah gets a marketing job at a small business. She's excited about her new job but is at a loss on what to do with a mountain of student loan debt, about $25,000. She doesn't really want to think about it though and would rather drown her high debt pain by purchasing a new German luxury coupe. She loves her new ride, but as time goes by, her happiness diminishes. What doesn't diminish is her $600 per month car note. She wants to move out of her parent's basement but feels trapped. There is no way she can afford a place with over $1000 in debt payments plus all the expense for the car and food.

John lands a job as an engineer at a firm just outside of Washington D.C. His new firm offers a defined contribution plan in the form of a Fidelity administered 401k. John has about the same amount of student loan debt as Sarah, but he decides to enroll in his company's 401k plan shortly after his hire date. He's happy with his new job. He's making money, living in his own place, and investing in a 401k plan. John decides, through Fidelity, that he'd like to invest in bonds. After all, he saw his parents lose big in the Great Recession of 2008-2009. He is smarter than that; he invests prudently in low yielding bonds and doesn't worry about the fluctuations of the equity market. John proudly proclaims to his coworkers that he's investing and that he'll be rich one day.

Sarah can't stand being dependent on her parents for a place to live. She's been listening to Dave Ramsey and is getting fed up with being in debt. She decides to get "weird". She runs her credit cards through the shredder, sells her car, and sets her sights on eliminating her student loan debt. She attacks her debt over the next two years and is able to eliminate all of her debt. She still lives at home but is saving more now than ever. She couldn't be happier in her ten-year-old Honda, saving money on insurance, gas, and maintenance.

John, on the other hand, is getting frustrated. His prudent investment strategy is losing efficacy with each passing month. He read the prospectus on his bond fund and checked out the different multi-year returns, but he didn't read the part about past performance not guaranteeing future results. Bonds are supposed to yield several percent a year. They're not supposed to go down in value! Rising interest rates are killing John's bond funds but he doesn't know why it's happening.

Now that her debt is eliminated, Sarah decides to put some cash to work in stocks. She's not sure why, but she prefers dividend paying stocks. She's risk averse and likes the idea of mature companies giving their shareholders money. The cash she receives on a quarterly basis seems like it's too good to be true. The more she puts to work in dividend paying stocks, the more she *wants* to put in dividend paying stocks. She finds out pretty soon that her dividends are able to pay for a new car payment. She passes. Instead, she reinvests her dividends back into the stocks she already owns.

Life goes on for John and Sarah. After some time, Sarah's net worth exceeds that of John. John thought he was doing everything right but he wasn't educated about the market.

The graph below shows John and Sarah's net worth through time. Sarah starts out with a larger debt, but is able to breakeven at year four and a half. John's more "conservative" but ill-advised investment in bonds makes his breakeven point at eight years. Sarah's investment in dividend growth stocks allows her investments to expand exponentially, instead of linearly like John's.

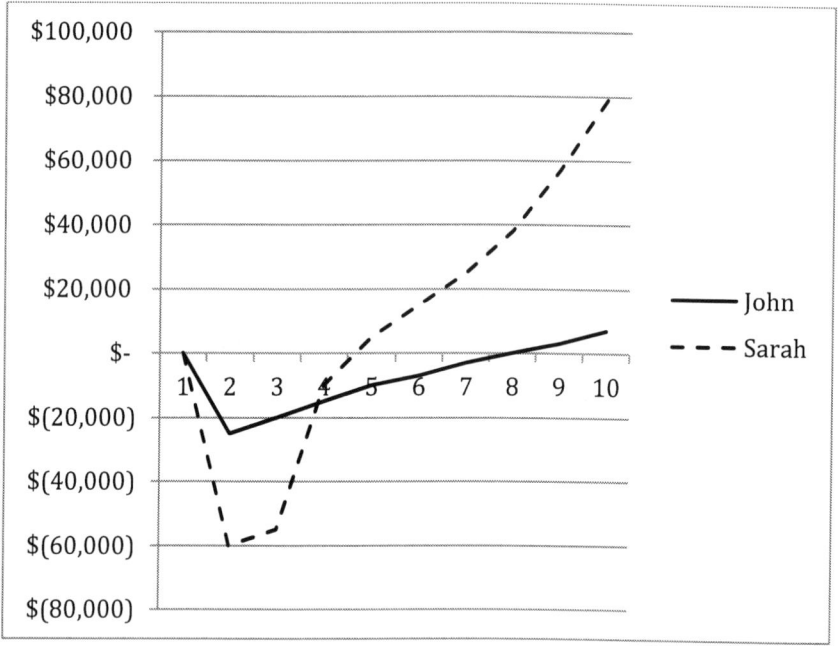

Compound Growth

What makes it possible for you to live off dividends is simple. Dividends grow at an exponential rate of growth. That means that instead of getting paid $1.00 in year 1, $1.10 in year 2, and $1.20 in year 3 (linear growth), you get paid $1.00 in year 1, $1.10 in year 2, and $1.21 in year 3 (compound growth). Here's a chart that shows this effect:

Year	Linear	Compound
1	$1.00	$1.00
2	$1.10	$1.10
3	$1.20	$1.21
4	$1.30	$1.33
5	$1.40	$1.46
6	$1.50	$1.61
7	$1.60	$1.77
8	$1.70	$1.95
9	$1.80	$2.14
10	$1.90	$2.36
11	$2.00	$2.59
12	$2.10	$2.85
13	$2.20	$3.14
14	$2.30	$3.45
15	$2.40	$3.80

In year 15, dividends of $3.80 will be paid out under the 10 percent compound growth model. That's almost four times the original dividend amount. In the early years, the differences are small and may almost seem too insignificant to be of any consequence. Over time, the differences between the two rates of growth are much more salient.

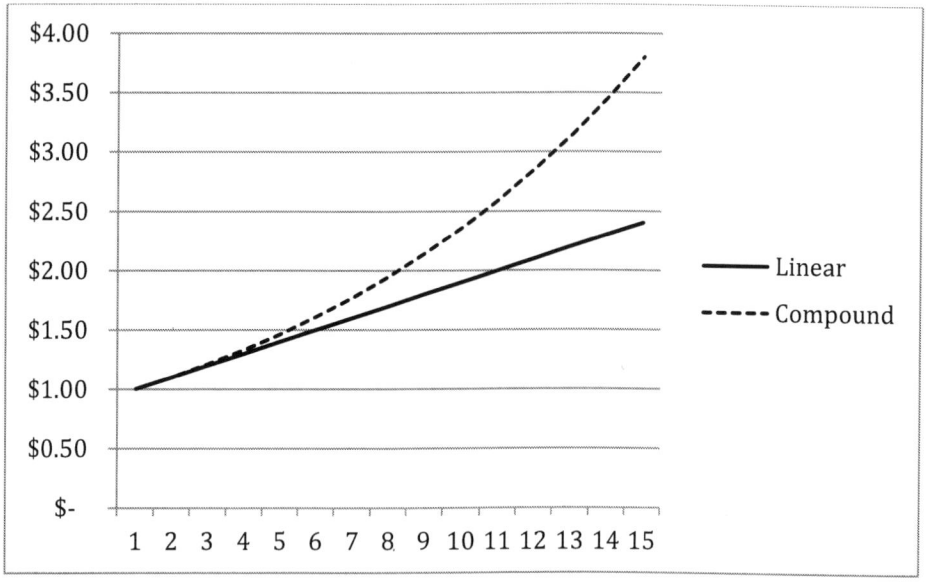

It is also important to know the distinction between compound and simple growth rates to calculate rates of return. Most novice investors will say that they made 10 percent per year if their stock is up 100 percent over 10 years. Seems simple enough but it couldn't be more wrong. The rate of return is actually 7.18 percent compounded annually. In finance, this is called the CAGR (Compound Annual Growth Rate).

Year	Stock Price
0	$10.00
1	$10.72
2	$11.49
3	$12.31
4	$13.20
5	$14.14
6	$15.16
7	$16.25
8	$17.41
9	$18.66
10	$20.00

You can also remember this by using the "Rule of 72". The Rule of 72 states: at a rate of 10 percent, your money will double every 7.2 years. You can also flip the two inputs around. At a rate of 7.2 percent, your money will double every 10 years. It's an easy way to compute rates in year head using this rule. As dividend growth investors, we're looking for companies that grow dividends at 10 percent per year. Given the Rule of 72, your dividends will double every 7.2 years. It will double again in another 7.2 years, and again.

Chapter 2

Diversification and Allocation

It is said that diversification is an investor's only "free lunch" - that is to say, there is no negative or cost to diversifying. As a dividend stock investor, I generally agree with this statement. It is unlikely that one holding in the portfolio will greatly affect the entire diversified portfolio. We're not chasing hot stocks and putting all of our capital into two or three companies. We'll leave that to the amateurs. Our goal is to have many dividend stocks paying us throughout the year.

How many stocks are enough? A study by Elton and Gruber found that the benefits to diversifying diminish after an investor has twenty stocks in his portfolio. I agree with this study but will extrapolate on Elton and Gruber's data. After holding just twelve stocks, in fact, most of the benefits of diversification are maximized.

A good way to look at this is to look at the standard deviation (sigma) of an entire portfolio as stocks are added. To show this point, you can look at portfolios which have different numbers of stocks in them. If an investor only has one stock in his portfolio, then the standard deviation of his portfolio has a wider range than the S&P 500. For the mean, use the S&P 500 index. It's the simplest index fund to find data for and it's the most prevalent source to reference against.

Over the course of any 12-month period, the S&P 500 index has a 68% (one standard deviation) chance of returning between a gain of 34.1% and a loss of 9.8%. This is an accurate statistical measurement which has been tested. However, that doesn't mean that the S&P can't lose 90% in one year, but that would be considered a high sigma event and is unlikely (more on that soon).

A one stock portfolio may have a 68% chance of returning

between a gain of 50% and a loss of 30%. This is hypothetical; all stocks have different returns related to standard deviation. To diversify away from this chance of a large loss, the investor must add another stock to his portfolio. Now with two stocks, there is a 68% chance of returning a gain of 45% and a loss of 25%. Notice how the gain and loss are both trimmed. The investor's risk went down and with it his expected return also went down. As you keep adding stocks, the expected gain and loss go down. This happens quite rapidly until you hold about ten stocks in your portfolio. As you add additional stocks to your portfolio beyond ten, the marginal benefit of diversification decreases rapidly. So much so that there is little benefit to diversifying after you hold twenty stocks in your portfolio.

There are two different costs to over-diversifying your portfolio. One is that transaction costs increase and may start to impact your overall performance. This is rare, but imagine you had to liquidate your positions. If you hold 100 different stocks, it may cost you close to $1,000 just in commissions to sell your holdings. The second cost is the inability to keep track of far too many stocks in your portfolio. Maybe the number you can keep track of is higher than twenty, that's great, but you're the rare investor indeed. Given the proof that there is little added benefit to keeping more than twenty stocks, retaining between twelve and twenty stocks unquestionably becomes the sweet spot of diversification.

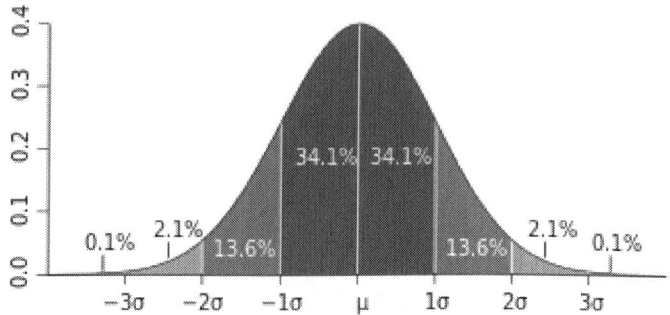

It's fitting in a section where we talk about sigma to also talk about high-sigma events also know as "black swans". Credit goes to Nassim Taleb, a New York University professor, for his work on the subject of unlikely events that are all too common. His main point is that financial models leave out the risks that cannot be predicted. Lehman Brothers is a great example of this. Analysts forecasted five years of financial data for Lehman Brothers two months before they went bankrupt. An investor could look at the analysts' forecast and think, "wow, what a great investment, look at the pretty charts that keep going up and up." Then this investor buys one thousand shares at what he believes to be a great price, and two months later he is begging his wife not to divorce him for being such a dumb investor.

> *"There are things we know that we know. There are some things we know we don't know. Then there are some things that we don't know that we don't know."* ~Donald Rumsfeld

This all may sound like gibberish at first glance, but any student of philosophy could make sense of this gibberish faster than most philosophical writings (Hegel is especially known for writing incoherent gibberish). Rumsfeld was, of course, speaking about terrorist attacks and threats to America, but this analytical statement can also be used in the world of finance and investing. There are things that investment professionals know they know. For example, finance professionals know that a dividend will make a quarterly payment as long as cash flow is sufficient to cover it. Then there are things like short-term stock price movements, which they know they don't know (even if they say they do). Then there are the fat tails of the investment world that can't be seen. There are certain things that no one person can predict. These "unknown unknowns" happen from time to time and they are totally unpredictable. Taleb has popularized these as black swans.

Beta

When discussing diversification, it's also important to include another statistical measure called beta. Beta is generally considered to be a risk measure of an individual stock or a portfolio of stocks. It measures the volatility between an asset and all investable assets. Instead of using "all investable assets", as it's hard to get data on this, most use the S&P 500 as the proxy to measure beta.

The S&P 500 will always have a beta of 1. If a stock has a beta of 2, then it will increase or decrease twice as much as the S&P 500 (on average). If the S&P 500 moves 2% in a day, you can expect a 2-beta stock to move 4%. This is great if the market is moving up, greater risk, higher returns. What if the market moves down? You may remember in the Great Recession of 2008-2009, many of the high beta high growth stocks cratered. During that time period, financials were hardest hit, followed by anything with a higher beta. It should also be noted that many of the stocks that performed the worst during the Great Recession also recovered quickly when the market pivoted in March of 2009.

As a dividend investor, most of the stocks in our universe have a low beta. A typical dividend stock has a beta of between 0.5 and 1. This means the typical stock will move less than the market moves in either direction. This is great in a down market, but dividend investing can be hard to stick with during an extended bull market. Few investors were talking about their dividend stocks during the great technology boom of the late 1990's. The stocks that were going up and up were names like Amazon, Microsoft, and Pets.com, the latter of which had a hard time making a profit and went bankrupt rather quickly after the crash of March 2000. If you told your day-trading neighbor that you were invested in Proctor and Gamble and Johnson & Johnson during the tech boom, he would have been perplexed by your idiocy. Your investing prescience would be rewarded, however, as your day-trading neighbor went back to work in March of 2000.

It's also worth noting that dividends aren't in the calculation of beta. If the market is going up and your dividend portfolio is lagging behind, remember that you also have dividends coming into your account that add to your total return. Not only do you have dividends coming in, your dividends are growing every year. Over the long haul, a diversified and properly allocated dividend portfolio will outperform the S&P 500 index. Every metric that you look at shows this fact. According to Bloomberg, dividends have accounted for 40% of total stock market return since 1988.

There are three main variables that drive the market:

1. Dividend growth

2. Earnings growth

3. Price to earnings expansion (multiple expansion)

The first two factors are what the dividend investor should focus on. The last factor, Price to earnings expansion, also known as P/E expansion, is based on the overall feelings of market participants. As you are probably aware, "feelings" are a difficult thing to forecast in your financial modeling. In fact, Warren Buffet prefers the "Mr. Market" metaphor. He's unsure of what Mr. Market will do on any given day, week, or month. Mr. Market is moody. His bi-polar behavior produces wild swings in the market to which the astute investor can take advantage of. If Mr. Market goes into a deep depression, P/E ratios will be compressed and the overall market will go down. Yet, many will tell you that the market is efficient, properly discounting a multitude of variables to come up with the perfect price.

Portfolio Allocation

One of the most difficult aspects for the novice investor to figure out is portfolio allocation. Allocation of capital is a difficult, yet highly rewarded in our capitalist society. The reason why successful entrepreneurs are rewarded so heavily is their ability to allocate capital wisely. Sure, they work hard too, but many people work hard and are not rewarded financially. Many people work hard for a company all year long, the outcome being that they are given a meager increase in their wage, which may not even be greater than the rate of inflation.

As a dividend investor, our goal is to eventually invest in twenty companies that generate ever-increasing dividend and earnings growth. Starting out, you may not be able to invest in twenty different companies. If you have $5,000 to start with, you may be able to invest in no more than five different companies, depending on the commissions that you're paying on each trade. You should not pay more than 0.5 percent to own a stock. For example, if you have $1,000 to allocate to a stock, you should not pay more than $5 in commissions for this trade. Of course, as your portfolio and capital grows, you want your commission percentage to drop significantly. I recommend a 0.2 percent commission on each trade as your capital grows. That would mean that for a $3,000 trade, you spend no more than $7 in commissions.

The weighting of each stock in your portfolio doesn't have to be equal, but there shouldn't be huge variations. For example, if one stock in your portfolio accounts for 30% and each of the rest of your stocks account for 5 percent, then your portfolio is not allocated properly. Here's an example of a sound twenty stock portfolio:

TICKER	AMOUNT INVESTED	PERCENTAGE OF PORTFOLIO
PM	$6,000.00	6.00%
O	$5,200.00	5.20%
SO	$4,000.00	4.00%
MCD	$6,000.00	6.00%
KRFT	$5,000.00	5.00%
CAG	$3,500.00	3.50%
KO	$6,000.00	6.00%
PEP	$6,000.00	6.00%
T	$4,800.00	4.80%
VZ	$4,000.00	4.00%
MO	$5,000.00	5.00%
DUK	$4,500.00	4.50%
KMP	$6,000.00	6.00%
KMI	$4,500.00	4.50%
EPD	$5,000.00	5.00%
PG	$5,000.00	5.00%
JNJ	$4,500.00	4.50%
LMT	$5,700.00	5.70%
COP	$5,300.00	5.30%
KMB	$4,000.00	4.00%

If any one stock collapses during the time you're holding it, it will not be catastrophic if your portfolio is allocated properly. Notice that each stock represents between 3.5 and 6.0 percent. This is a good goal to shoot for after you have a large number of stocks in your portfolio. This also means that if one stock increases substantially, the increase in your overall portfolio will be limited. The dividend growth investor is not concerned with making huge price appreciations, but rather a reliable stream of growing dividends.

The Dumbbell Approach to Asset Allocation

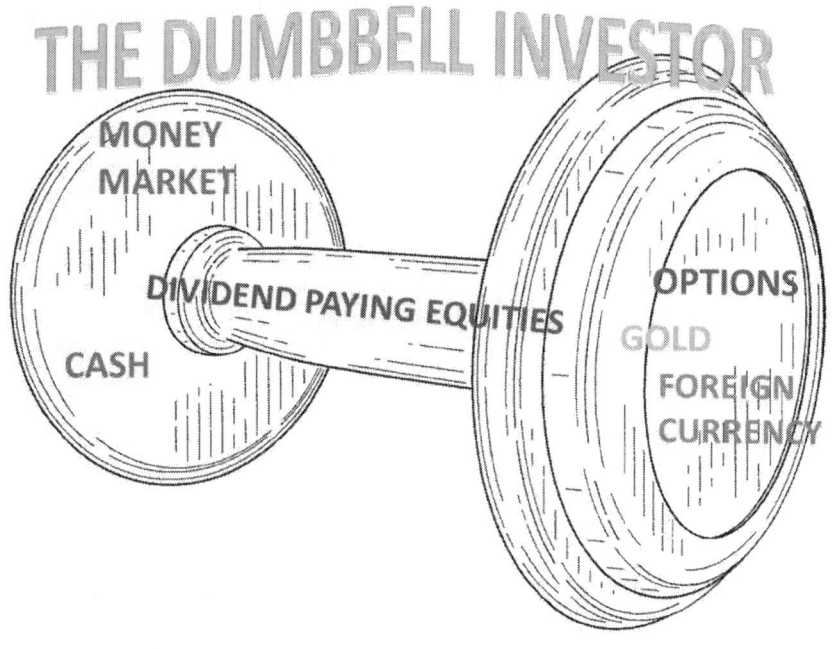

You may have heard of the term "barbell investing." It was originally used to describe a bond portfolio that contained very short-term bonds (low risk) and very long-term bonds (higher risk). I use the term "dumbbell investing" to mean the allocation of an investor's entire portfolio of assets. It's a good way to describe a style that has three different investable asset classes:

1. Cash or Money Market Funds (low risk)
2. Dividend Paying Equities (medium risk)
3. Precious Metals, Options, Foreign Currency (high risk)

If you look at the dumbbell, it has three different areas that are analogous to the risk curve. You have safe investments on the left side, medium-risk assets in the middle, and high-risk assets on the right side. The allocation percentage to each of these asset classes is up to each individual investor, but dividend-paying stocks should make up the majority (50 – 80 percent). The rest should be split up between cash and high-risk assets like gold. Gold is a great hedge against market downturns, but it doesn't generate a cash flow, thus is difficult to value. You could also buy small amounts of put-option contracts on the S&P 500 index to insure your portfolio against downside risk. This option is more appealing as the market gets higher and higher.

If you're just starting your portfolio, the best dividend stocks you can buy are the big well-known companies listed in the following chapters of this book. A novice dividend investor should start with normal equity investments. As you progress, then proceed to buy REITs (real estate investments trusts) and MLPs (master limited partnerships) only if you feel comfortable. There are risks and tax consequences when purchasing REITs and MLPs that we'll go over in Chapter 23. A company like Philip Morris International (PM) is my favorite stock to start a dividend stock portfolio with (see Chapter 3). The next 20 chapters in this book give an analysis of the top 20 stocks that you can buy in 2014.

Chapter 3

Philip Morris International

Philip Morris International Inc., (Ticker: PM) is a holding company consisting of Philip Morris' subsidiaries and affiliates. Their licensees are engaged in the manufacture and sale of cigarettes and other tobacco products in markets outside of the United States. Its products are sold in approximately 180 countries. The key is that Philip Morris International Inc. sells its products outside of the United States, away from onerous U.S. government restrictions that could hamper their business.

Tobacco companies generally trade at lower P/E ratios than stocks in other industries. It's not uncommon to see P/E ratios around 15, which is relatively low. Many tobacco companies have large liabilities related to previous litigation. The negative factors are priced into this company's stock price, which is why you see a compressed P/E ratio.

However, the company could not be more generous to its shareholders, and this means you have to own it. It's one of the best dividend stocks that you can find today. Not only does the company payout about 65 percent of its earnings to shareholders, it also has bought back billions of dollars worth of it stock since 2008. The company believes that its shares are attractively valued and between 2008 and the end of 2013 bought back one third of the company. That means that every share of stock that you own gives you a bigger share of the company's earnings potential.

If you invested $10,000 in this stock at the beginning of 2009 (its first full year of trading), it would be worth $18,812 in 2014. During that time, the company would have paid you $3,245 in dividends. That represents a five-year return of 121 percent (CAGR 8.23 percent). So, in the first half of 2014, the company has paid out $0.94 per quarter, and your initial $10,000 investment in Philip Morris would have given you a current yield of 8.5 percent. In other words, you would have more than doubled your money between 2009 and 2014, as well as acquired an increasing stream of quarterly dividend payments.

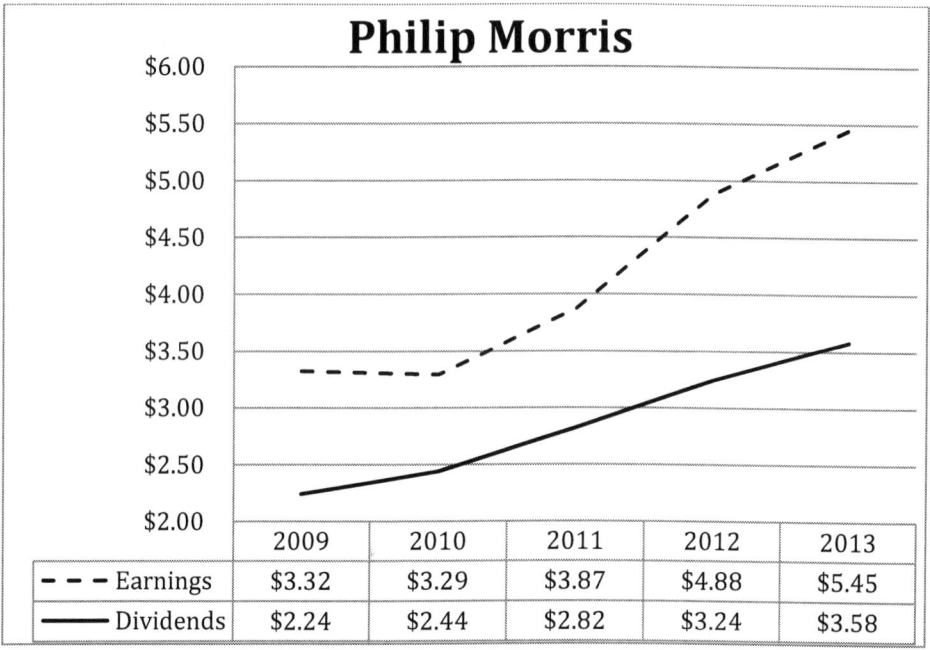

In the future, you can expect Philip Morris to raise its dividend at a rate of 10 percent per year. At this rate, PM manages to double its dividend payment about every seven and a half years. In the year 2022, the annual dividend payment will be about $8.50. The investor that purchases Philip Morris in 2014 will have a dividend yield of over 10 percent in 2022.

It's imperative for the dividend investor to think long term. While the year 2022 may sound like it's in the distance future, it's not. Keeping a long-term outlook will help you withstand the vicissitudes of Mr. Market. It's one of the many advantages that the individual investor has – not to have your portfolio performance graded every quarter. You can relax knowing that you have companies out there making you money while you work on other more creative endeavors. In fact, it would be wise for you not to check stock quotes on more than a quarterly basis once you purchased the stock. Focus on your next investment and buying it at the right price.

Chapter 4

Realty Income Corporation

Realty Income Corporation (Ticker: O) is an equity real estate investment trust (REIT). As such, it's more favorable to own this in a tax-deferred account. The Company is engaged in acquiring and owning freestanding retail and other properties that generate rental revenue under long-term lease agreements (primarily 10 plus years). On December 31, 2013, it owned a diversified portfolio of over 3800 properties with an occupancy rate of 98.1%. Its properties are located in 49 states, having tenants with a broad industry diversification.

Due to its size, operations, and management, this company is the best real estate investment trust you can own. It is one of the largest REITs on the market having a total market capitalization of $13 billion. Of that total market capitalization, $8 billion is made up of equity, while debt and preferred stock makes up the remainder. It successfully maintains a conservative balance sheet, one of managements' long-term goals.

Realty Income uses the triple net lease model for its rental operations. This is a brilliant way to own and rent property. This type of lease requires the lessee to pay for net real estate taxes on the leased building, net building insurance and net common area maintenance. The tenants of these properties include Coca Cola, FedEx, International Paper, Walgreen Co., Cinemark, T-Mobile, Caterpillar, LA Fitness, and others.

Imagine you're a landlord. You own some property and would like to rent it out. You put an ad in the paper or online and get a few calls. When you meet with the prospective tenant, you tell her that she would be responsible for the real estate taxes, the property insurance, and she has to mow the lawn and shovel the snow. She would run away as fast as she could. There's no way you could do this type of deal in the personal residence real estate world. But in the business world, Realty Income does this for each and every deal.

The benefits of triple net leases don't cease with having your tenant pay for everything. Realty Income is protected from inflating property taxes and insurance premiums. As local governments strive to maintain fiscal balance, they may increase property taxes, but that's not an issue if you've written a triple net lease agreement. The tenant would pay for any increase in property taxes, not the owner.

REITs tend to be hurt by a rising interest rate environment. In fact, market participants sold off REITs in general in the middle of 2013. REITs were performing very well in early 2013, then as interest rates shot up in mid-2013, REITs sold off extraordinarily. Realty income was no exception to this broad sell-off. However, over the long haul, investors will be compensated in inflationary or deflationary times. Realty Income has generally performed well in both inflationary and deflationary scenarios.

On the inflationary side, Realty Income is protected from increasing property expenses because of their net lease structure. They may not be able to increase rents fast enough to cover rising inflation due to their long-term lease agreements. Further, it is a generally held belief that owning real estate during inflation is a hedge against inflation since property values will go up (and eventually rents will follow). On the deflationary side, Realty Income is protected because of their long-term lease agreements. As prices trend lower during deflation, rents will continue to increase during the life of the lease.

Albert Einstein said that the power of compounding interest is one of the most powerful forces in the universe. Realty Income pays their dividend on a monthly basis, therefore compounding at a greater rate than the normal quarterly paid dividends. You get paid each and every month if you own Realty Income's stock. On the 15th of each month, you'll receive a dividend payment to your account, which you can use to reinvest or hold in cash until you see other investing opportunities.

In 2014, Realty Income is paying a 5.7 percent dividend or about $2.20 per share. Realty Income increases dividend distributions frequently but at a low rate of increase. There was a big increase in the dividend payment in 2013, but this was due to the acquisition of another REIT.

Since Realty Income is a real estate investment trust, it's required by law to pay out most of net income as dividends (at least 90%). That may seem like a lot at first glance, but remember that net earnings are net of depreciation and amortization, which is a huge non-cash expense for real estate companies.

Instead of using Earnings Per Share (EPS), it's more practical for REITs to use Funds From Operation (FFO). We'll use FFO in the chart below and compare it to dividends paid since 2009. As you can see, Realty Income has a high FFO to dividend payout ratio. This is not uncommon for a REIT. Most REITS finance expansion through the use of equity and debt, not retained earnings. If this were a chain of big box stores, it would be a big negative to have such a high payout ratio. It would signal problems and the dividend would likely be cut in the near future. This is not the case with REITs, however, and you have to remember that popular ratios like P/E are generally garbage.

Realty Income

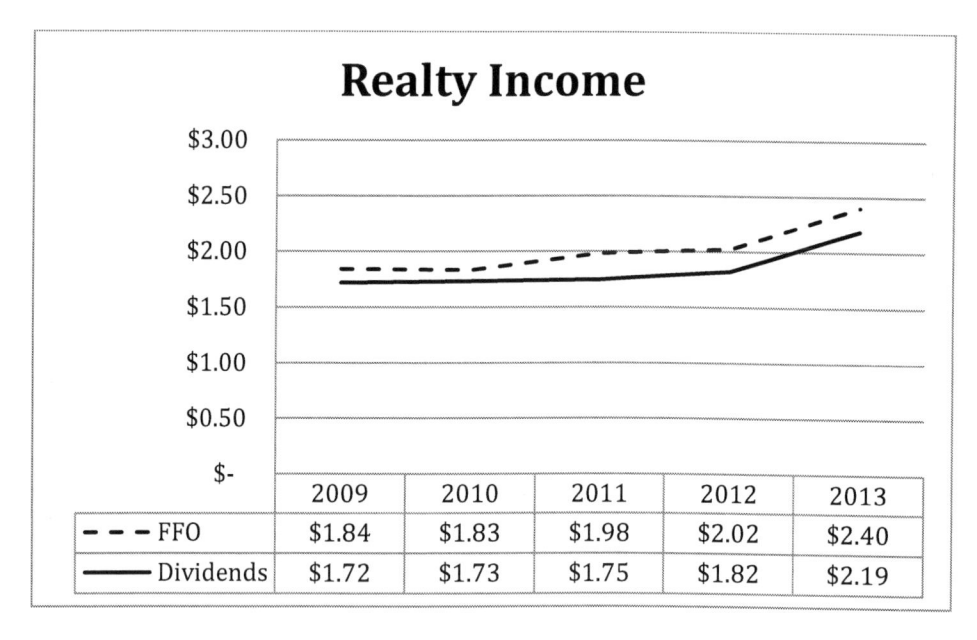

	2009	2010	2011	2012	2013
- - - FFO	$1.84	$1.83	$1.98	$2.02	$2.40
—— Dividends	$1.72	$1.73	$1.75	$1.82	$2.19

If you invested $10,000 in this stock at the beginning of 2009, it would be worth $19,250 in 2014. During that time, the company would have paid you $4,600 in dividends. That represents a five-year return of 238 percent. In the first half of 2014, the company is paying out $0.1822 per month in dividends. Your initial $10,000 investment in Realty Income would be giving you a current yield of 11 percent.

I first purchased Realty Income in 2008 for its 6 percent dividend yield. I didn't know how well the company was run and how seriously they take their dividends. I was impressed by the changes the company made during that time and how they got through the credit crisis of 2008 virtually unscathed. What a great time it was to buy back then. The next greatest time to buy this stock is today.

I would buy Realty Income as long as it's trading below 18 times its price to FFO ratio. If the 10-year Treasury bond yield increases in 2014, Realty Income's market price could drop more. This would be a perfect buying opportunity for the long-term investor.

Chapter 5

The Southern Company

The Southern Company (Ticker: SO) is a holding company which owns all of the common stock of the following: Alabama Power Company, Georgia Power Company, Gulf Power Company, Mississippi Power Company, and Southern Power Company. It is the utility company of the South. The operating companies are vertically integrated utilities providing electric service in four Southeastern states. In early 2014, The Southern Company is in the process of constructing a new coal plant in Mississippi that will be the cleanest coal plant in America.

The Southern Company is the utility stock you have to have in your portfolio in 2014 and beyond. The stock trades at just above $40 per share and sports a 5 percent dividend yield. It's currently discounted in the marketplace because of its poor performance during 2013. The Southern Company had issues with one of its coal gasification plants in Mississippi. It costs the company over $600 million in after-tax charges, which directly affected the bottom line.

This is of little importance to the long-term investor and providers a great opportunity to buy into a great utility at a low price. Since theses charges will mostly affect the 2013 fiscal year, earnings will bounce back in 2014. The temporary earnings decrease did not affect dividends. The company continues to pay and even increase dividends during trying times. This suggests that management is confident that cash flow is adequate to cover dividends and earnings will bounce back in 2014.

The Southern Company

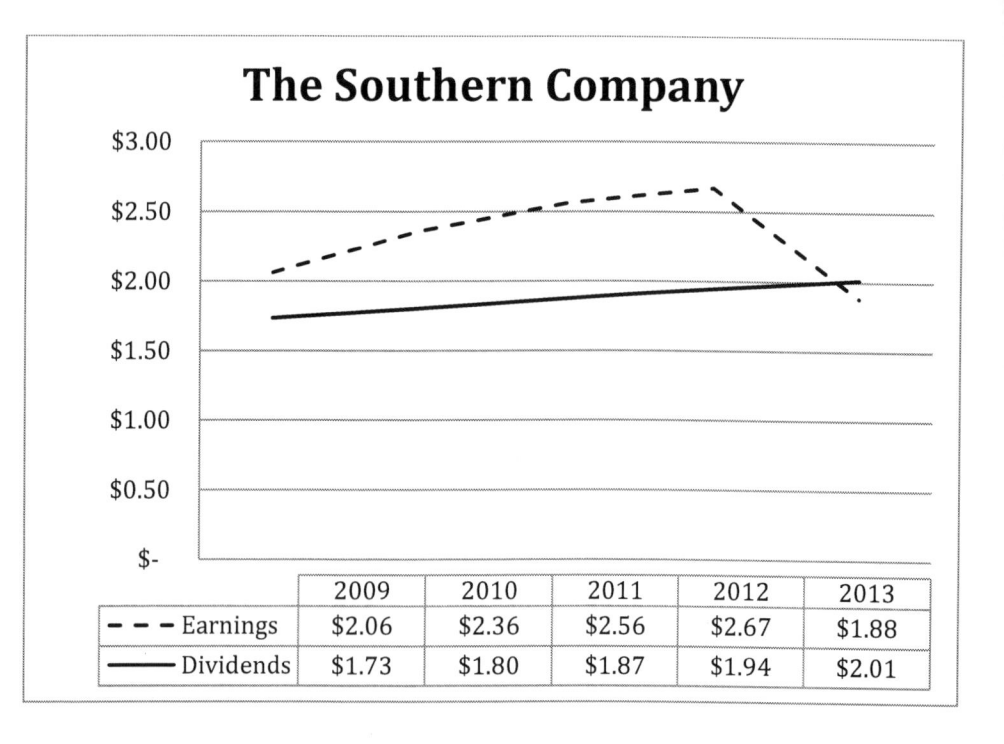

	2009	2010	2011	2012	2013
--- Earnings	$2.06	$2.36	$2.56	$2.67	$1.88
—— Dividends	$1.73	$1.80	$1.87	$1.94	$2.01

If you invested $10,000 in this stock at the beginning of 2009, it would be worth $11,066 in 2014. During that time, the company would have paid you $2,500 in dividends. The gain in principle plus dividends for 5 years gives you a return of 35 percent. In the first half of 2014, the company is paying out $0.51 per quarter. Your initial $10,000 investment in The Southern Company would give a current yield of 5.4 percent.

The past five years performance has been lackluster. During this time the company has put strategic assets to work and put an end to money losing capital projects like the coal gasification plant in Mississippi. The company has finally made it through a transition period, and earnings and dividend growth will accelerate in the years to come.

The patient investor in this utility can expect the next five years to be much better. With a dividend growth rate of 7 percent per annum, in 2018, this stock will be paying out a dividend of $2.82 per share.

A quick note on utilities: you can expect a higher current dividend yield with utilities but a lower dividend growth rate. You should still expect a growth rate in both dividends and earnings, and in the utility space, you should stay away from Exelon Corporation. Not only does it lose money for shareholders every year, it also had to cut its dividend in half. It may bounce back eventually, but its track record in the recent years has been very weak.

Chapter 6

McDonald's Corporation

McDonald's Corporation (Ticker MCD) franchises and operates McDonald's restaurants around the world in 119 countries. All restaurants are operated either by the company or by franchisees. McDonald's is the leader in fast food restaurant sales with approximately $28 billion in 2013. With a current yield of close to 3.5 percent in early 2014 and one of the fastest dividend growth rates for a mature company, this is a must have stock for your portfolio.

A close to 3.5 percent yield sounds good but what really makes it great is the growth rate. McDonald's is very shareholder friendly, increasing the cash it pays to shareholders at a rapid rate. The company has been increasing dividends by an average of 11 percent from 2009 to 2013. If you buy this stock in 2014 and hold it, you could expect dividends of $5.02 annually in 2018 (using an ambitious 10 percent growth rate). $5.02 per share in dividends would give you a yield on cost of 5.3 percent. A 10 percent growth rate translates into your dividend payment doubling every 7 years.

Not only does McDonald's focus on returning shareholder value through dividends, they also repurchase company stock on the open market aggressively. In the first nine months of 2013, McDonald's bought back well over $1 billion worth of its stock. This suggests that McDonald's management see the $95 share price as fairly or undervalued. Management returns about $2.5 billion back to shareholders each year through share repurchases. You can expect this to increase in the future as growth in restaurant count slows and McDonald's looks for ways to continually improve shareholder value.

McDonald's

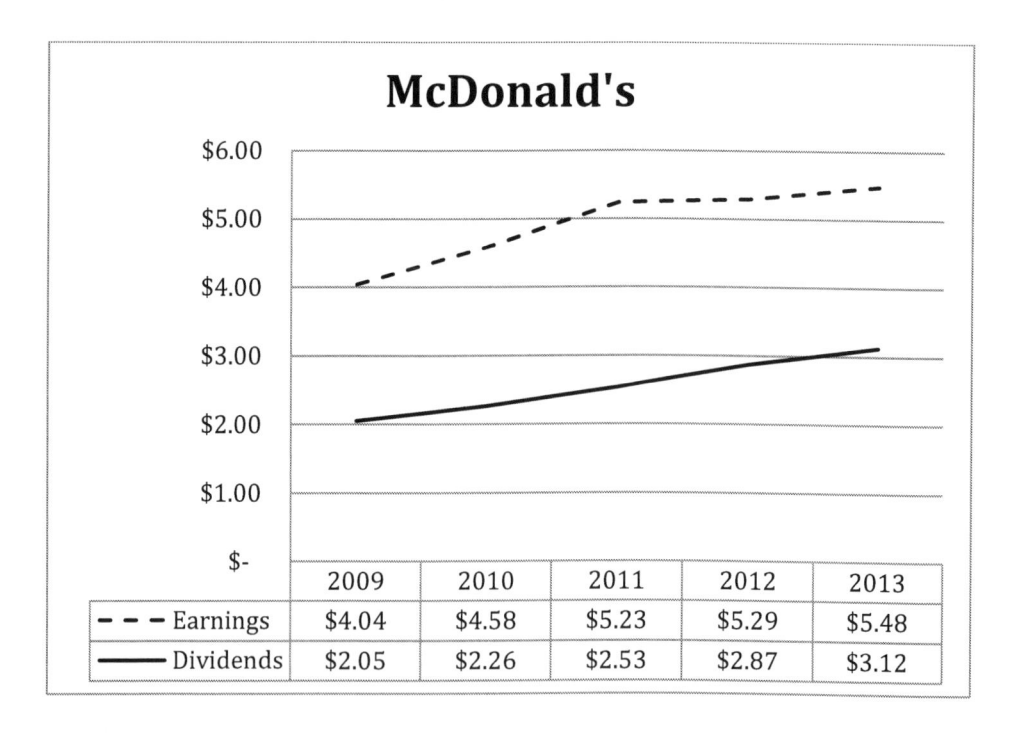

	2009	2010	2011	2012	2013
- - - Earnings	$4.04	$4.58	$5.23	$5.29	$5.48
—— Dividends	$2.05	$2.26	$2.53	$2.87	$3.12

As you can see in the chart above, the dividend payout ratio is conservative, usually running at about 50 percent of earnings. The growth in earnings is adequate to cover the high dividend growth rate of over 10 percent.

    I would buy McDonald's stock in 2014 at any price below $105 per share. The stock has consolidated around $95 share. You could have picked up shares of McDonald's at $95 back in late 2011 and $95 in early 2014. This may suggest that the stock is dead money. I disagree. I think investors aren't appreciating the growth potential of McDonald's. The company will only increase share repurchases and dividends in the future. Buying today guarantees that you'll get a piece of that growth in the future.

    Some worry that McDonald's sells food that may be going out of style due to the more health conscious consumer. I disagree with this also. McDonald's has shown that it will sell what people buy, whether it's a Big Mac or a Salad, whether it's fries or a fruit cup. The largest competitor to McDonald's will be

Chic-fil-A in the future. Chic-fil-A is the only fast food restaurant mimicking McDonald's business acumen: a competitive edge, a well-known brand, and great management. There will be room for both fast food companies in the world, but some of the other fast food restaurants should be worried.

Chapter 7

Kraft Foods Group Inc.

Kraft Foods Group Inc., (Ticker: KRFT) is the product of the 2012 spinoff of old Kraft where the company essentially split itself into two parts, Kraft Foods Group Inc., (KRFT) and Mondelēz International (MDLZ). Mondelēz contains the snack brands like Chips Ahoy! and Cadbury. The new Kraft Foods contains the North American food brands like Kraft Mayo and Oscar Mayer. The new Kraft has a slower growth rate but makes up for that with an almost 4 percent current dividend and a huge share buyback program in place. It's also attractively valued at 17 times 2013 earnings.

Kraft Foods is committed to returning shareholder value through dividends and its stock repurchase program. In December of 2013, Kraft announced that its Board of Directors had authorized a $3 billion stock repurchase program. That is a huge program for a company with a market capitalization of $32 billion. That's almost 10 percent of the entire company! With the scope of this repurchase program, Kraft will have to be in the market almost everyday buying millions of dollars of its own stock. You do not want to get on the wrong side of this move. Kraft will go higher, much higher over time, and its dividends will also grow at a healthy clip.

Since old Kraft spun off in 2012, it's difficult to analyze this newer company, KRFT. The above graph shows EPS and dividend data from 2012, 2013, and estimated data for 2014. Earnings are expected to grow at about 6 percent going forward, but with the massive share buyback program in place, I think earnings will grow even faster.

Kraft Foods

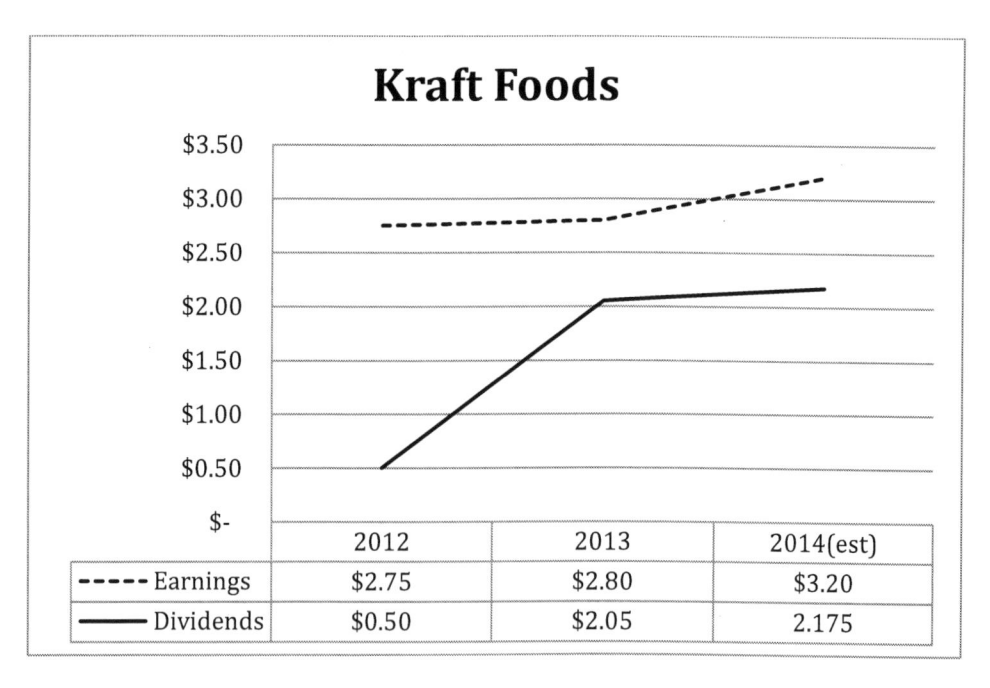

	2012	2013	2014(est)
----- Earnings	$2.75	$2.80	$3.20
——— Dividends	$0.50	$2.05	2.175

If you invest $10,000 into Kraft Foods in 2014, you can expect dividends of about $3.50 in 2019. This translates into a yield on original cost of 6.6 percent. You can also expect your original $10,000 investment to be worth $16,500 in 5 years ($5.15 in earnings x P/E of 17). That's a total return of $9,286 - almost double your money in 5 years. Of course, as a dividend growth investor, the most important part of the return is the ever-increasing dividend.

A total return of $9,286 on your original investment of $10,000 translates into a compounded annual growth rate of 14 percent. If you could achieve a 14 percent return on your money over 30 years, your original $10,000 investment would turn into more than $500,000. This is the kind of growth you need to achieve your goal of living off of the dividends in your portfolio. Kraft may not return 14 percent returns very long, but after growth slows, you'll be able to find other companies to allocate capital to.

One of the great things about owning a food company is that they're boring. Being boring is a virtue to the patient dividend growth investor. After you purchase shares in Kraft, you'll be able to sleep easy at night. Kraft's volatility is about half that of the S&P 500 index (a beta of 0.5). If the market tanks one day, you can expect your Kraft stock to be down about half as much. You won't have to tune into CNBC to check what the talking heads are discussing. You won't even have to check the stock quote on your computer.

Food companies are recession resistant, not recession proof. People, after all, have to eat. When times are tough, consumers cut back on discretionary purchases. They may cut out that trip to Ruth's Chris or Morton's Steakhouse, but their grocery buying habits are generally less curtailed. Pricing may come under pressure, especially with a consumer switch to private label goods. This is why Kraft, with its large branded goods segment, may not be totally recession proof. Brand loyalty however, tends to be fairly strong even in times of economic recession. Consumers will continue to buy Kraft Mayo and other brands even if there pay is cut. The Great Recession of 2008-2009 showed that Kraft can continue to sell branded food in an economic downturn, even increase sales of certain branded products. During good economic times and bad, you can expect Kraft to be a solid performer.

Chapter 8

ConAgra Foods

ConAgra Foods, Inc., (Ticker: CAG), is a packaged food company with widely recognized brands such as Banquet, Marie Callender's, Chef Boyarde, Egg Beaters, Healthy Choice, Hebrew National, Hunt's, Odom's Tennessee Pride, Orville Redenbacher's, PAM, Peter Pan, Reddi-wip, Slim Jim, Snack Pack, and others. The company claims to have food in 97 percent of American households, and I don't doubt it. Not only does ConAgra have a multitude of brands, it also has a huge private label business.

Recently, ConAgra purchased Ralcorp Holdings. The combined company is the largest producer of private label foods. The private label business will be responsible for significant sales and earnings growth in the next few years. Retailers have an incentive to add private labels to their shelves for a few simple reasons. Margins on private label are about 10 – 15 percent higher than national brands. Retailers can control pricing and private label branding much better, and many stores put a lot of emphasis on their own brands.

Trader Joe's and Costco are two of ConAgra's customers that focus on their own brands. Both Trader Joe's and Costco have had great success with their brands. Customers buy them more often than national brands when in their respective stores. Another big retailer that's starting to increase private label is Whole Foods. With retailers like this as customers of ConAgra, there will be many years of growth ahead.

ConAgra has a dividend yield of just above 3 percent and growing. From 2009 – 2013, ConAgra has managed to grow its dividend at a rate of 5.5 percent. At first, 5.5 percent seems like it's on the low side, but with the acquisition of Ralcorp, dividend growth should increase substantially. Going forward, dividend growth should be in the 8 – 10 percent range. $10,000 invested in ConAgra in 2014 will get you 312 shares. The current dividend on your $10,000 investment will be $315 annually. After five years, you can expect your dividend to increase to $507. After twenty years, you can expect your annual dividend to be over $2,000 annually.

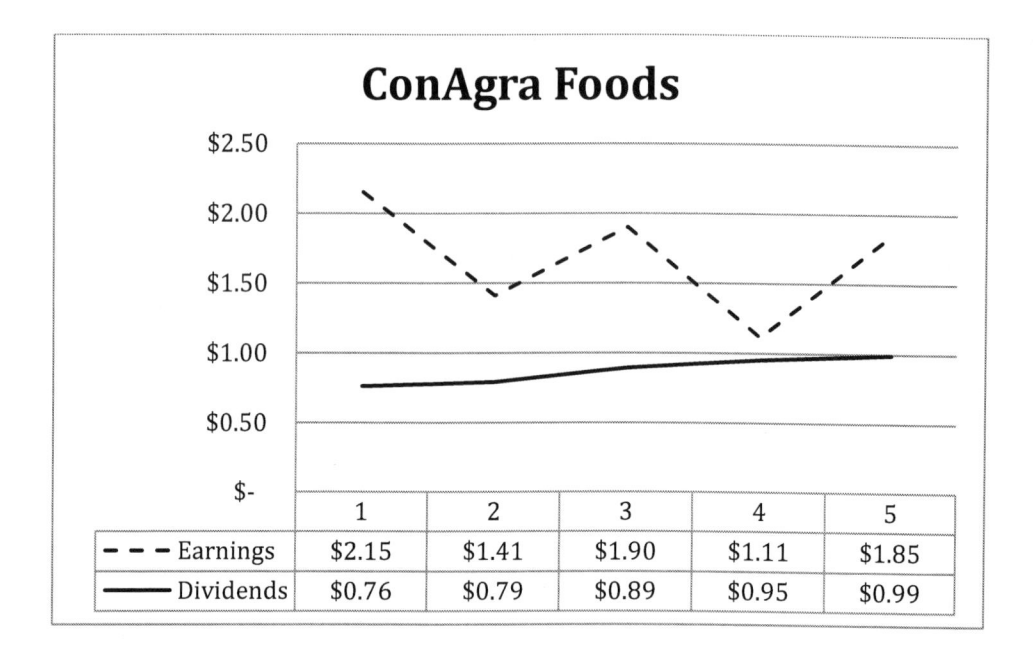

ConAgra Foods

	1	2	3	4	5
– – – Earnings	$2.15	$1.41	$1.90	$1.11	$1.85
——— Dividends	$0.76	$0.79	$0.89	$0.95	$0.99

ConAgra, like Kraft, is another great defensive stock. ConAgra has a big leg up on Kraft in that it controls the country's largest private label network. If consumers' taste preferences ever switch to store brands over branded items, ConAgra turns out to be a big winner. In a recession, expect this stock to perform better than most companies. In a boom economy, ConAgra will be able to grow sales and earnings at attractive rates.

Chapter 9

The Coca-Cola Company

The Coca-Cola Company (Ticker: KO), one of the world's best-known brands, owns or licenses and markets more than 500 nonalcoholic beverage labels. The beverages are primarily sparkling beverages but also a multitude of still beverages, such as waters, enhanced waters, juices and juice drinks, ready-to-drink teas and coffees, and energy and sports drinks.

One anecdote to point out the power of Coke: they pump water out of the ground and bottle it for a cost of about a dime, then sell it for over $1. Coke's Dasani brand of water is just behind PepsiCo's Aquafina brand with about 10 percent of the total bottled water market share. Behind Dasani and Aquafina is Glacéau Vitaminwater, which is also owned by Coke. The bottled water industry grossed a total of $11.8 billion in 2012, making bottled water about $1.22/gallon nationwide. That's 300 times the cost of a gallon of tap water! The beverage companies invented a new way to consume water, then branded it and sold it to the consumer at very high margins.

Some critics of "Big Soda" point out that soft drinks are on the decline. In the U.S., they would be correct, but they're on the rise outside of the U.S. Combine that with the fact that Coke buys almost every drink brand with growth, and you have a mature growth company that can afford to raise its dividend year after year.

Beverages bearing trademarks owned by or licensed to Coke account for over two billion servings daily. Their success depends on their ability to provide consumers with drinks that they want. Consumers' taste preferences change through time and Coke needs to be able to change with the consumer. Coke has been very successful in this endeavor and they're going into new brands and products every year.

Think about your interactions with Coke's brands through the years. You may have started out with regular Coca-Cola or Sprite. Then maybe you wanted to cut back on soda, so you decided to drink more Dasani water. Although you like bottled water now, you like something sweet from time to time. That's when you reach for a Glacéau Vitaminwater, which tastes like a light Gatorade type beverage. All along the way, whether you knew it or not, you were supporting Coke and in tern Coke's shareholders. Wouldn't it be nice to own part of the company that you're supporting? I think it's nice to own part of the company that you're a customer of, although it doesn't affect the actual stock price. You can imagine that every time you drink a Coke product, you're giving yourself a tiny dividend.

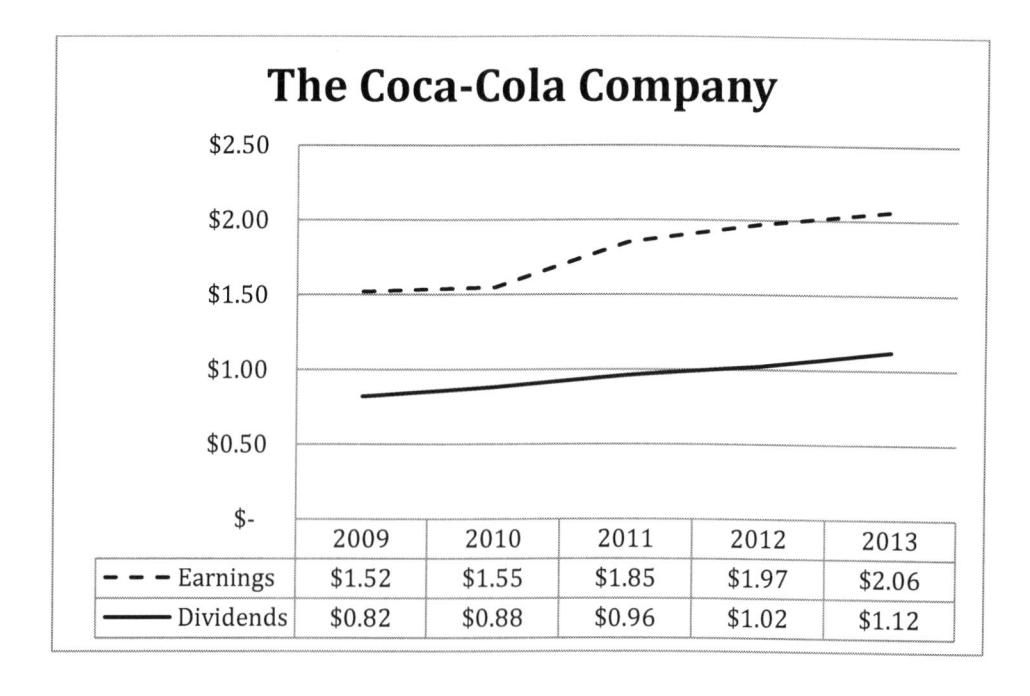

The Coca-Cola Company

	2009	2010	2011	2012	2013
Earnings	$1.52	$1.55	$1.85	$1.97	$2.06
Dividends	$0.82	$0.88	$0.96	$1.02	$1.12

Coke manages to grow earning and dividends steadily every year. Its 5-year dividend growth rate is 8.1 percent. That growth rate translates into Coke doubling its dividend close to every 8 years. If you invest $10,000 in Coke in 2014, your annual dividends will be $316. In 2019, you can expect Coke to pay you an annual dividend of $470 on your original $10,000 investment. An annual dividend of $470 translates into a yield on cost of 4.7 percent. After 20 years, you can expect Coke to pay you an annual dividend of $1,500.

In 2014, Coke signed a strategic agreement with Green Mountain Coffee Roasters. In the agreement Coke bought a 10 percent stake in Green Mountain in exchange for exclusive rights to all of the Keurig (Green Mountain's main drink system) cold beverages. What's great about this is that it will be a big growth catalyst for Coke. Management had the foresight to invest in a line of drinks that hasn't even been invented yet! The Keurig system has been a huge hit with consumers, and up until 2014 only hot beverages could be consumed. Keurig's cold system will use single-serve pods to dispense freshly-made cold beverages including carbonated drinks, enhanced waters, juice drinks, sports drinks and teas in consumers' homes. It may also be located in hotels and workplaces across America.

Chapter 10

PepsiCo, Inc.

PepsiCo, Inc. (Ticker: PEP) is a global food and beverage company. The company sells and distributes a range of foods and beverages in more than 200 countries and territories worldwide. PepsiCo is organized into four units of operation: PepsiCo Americas Foods, which includes Frito-Lay North America, Quaker Foods North America, and all of its Latin American food and snack businesses; PepsiCo Americas Beverages, which includes all of its Western Hemisphere beverage businesses; PepsiCo Europe, which includes all beverage, food and snack businesses in Europe and South Africa; and finally PepsiCo Asia, Middle East and Africa.

PepsiCo's brands are ubiquitous across the globe, with holdings such as Pepsi, Sun Chips, Cheetos, Quaker, Tropicana, Doritos, Stacy's, and many others. PepsiCo is a huge food company as well as a beverage company. CEO Indra Nooyi runs the company. She is an eclectic and driven leader, who has taken the company to a new level since her start there in 2006. In early 2014, there was a push by some investors to split the company into two parts: one beverage company and one food company. The Board of PepsiCo, however, rejected this in a vote. They apparently think that PepsiCo is better off as one big company. There may be advantages to splitting, like focusing competencies held by each distinct division, but this is likely overshadowed by the synergies the company has as one big company.

Like Coke, PepsiCo has a big business in selling water through the brand name Aquafina. As of 2014, Aquafina controlled the largest market share of bottled water at 10.3 percent. That doesn't sound like a lot, but when you consider how large and competitive the bottled water market is, 10.3 percent is a very large amount for a single brand. Consider the fact that there are literally dozens of bottled water brands and private labels. Think of all the choices you have in bottled water at your grocery store; Aquafina is doing quite well. In comparison, a very popular bottled water brand, Deer Park, has only 3.8 percent of the bottled water market share.

Gatorade is another successful PepsiCo brand. Gatorade was purchased with Quaker Oats in 2001 and now represents PepsiCo's fourth largest brand by global sales volume. Gatorade competes with Coke's Powerade and Vitaminwater. Gatorade underwent a rebranding starting in 2008. You may have noticed brands labeled G2 or Gatorade Rain at your local grocery store. This was PepsiCo's successful attempt to expand the brand to a wider consumer audience.

PepsiCo also makes money off bottling and distributing beverages for other companies. PepsiCo does this with Starbucks coffee drinks like DoubleShot, Frappuccino, and Iced Coffee. Starbucks doesn't have the facilities to do its own bottling so it turns to PepsiCo for this task. Starbucks makes money off of their brand, and PepsiCo makes money off the bottling and distribution aspect of the business. It's a perfect and profitable partnership.

Traditionally, PepsiCo's soda syrup business accounts for less sales volume but higher profits. Its bottled and canned soda business accounts for greater sales volume but lower profits. They have a good mix of both types of business. PepsiCo just defeated Coke in providing the restaurant chain Buffalo Wild Wings with soda, but Coke is still available in a greater number of restaurant chains. Pepsi is in Taco Bell, Pizza Hut, KFC, Panera Bread, as well as a few other chains. Coke is available in more than 23 chains. Coke still dominates the restaurant chain soda business, but PepsiCo just won a big battle in Buffalo Wild Wings.

PepsiCo has rewarded shareholders handsomely in the past five years. $10,000 invested in PepsiCo in 2009 would have turned into $14,500 in 2014. During that time, PepsiCo would have paid out $1,827 in dividends (that's without dividends being reinvested!). The total five-year return for PepsiCo was 10.3 percent from 2009 – 2013. PepsiCo's five-year dividend growth rate is a relatively low 6.0 percent; however, the company announced that it would raise dividends by 15 percent in 2014. Dividend growth should start to increase in 2014 and continue into the future. Over the next five years, expect PepsiCo's dividend growth rate to be about 12 percent.

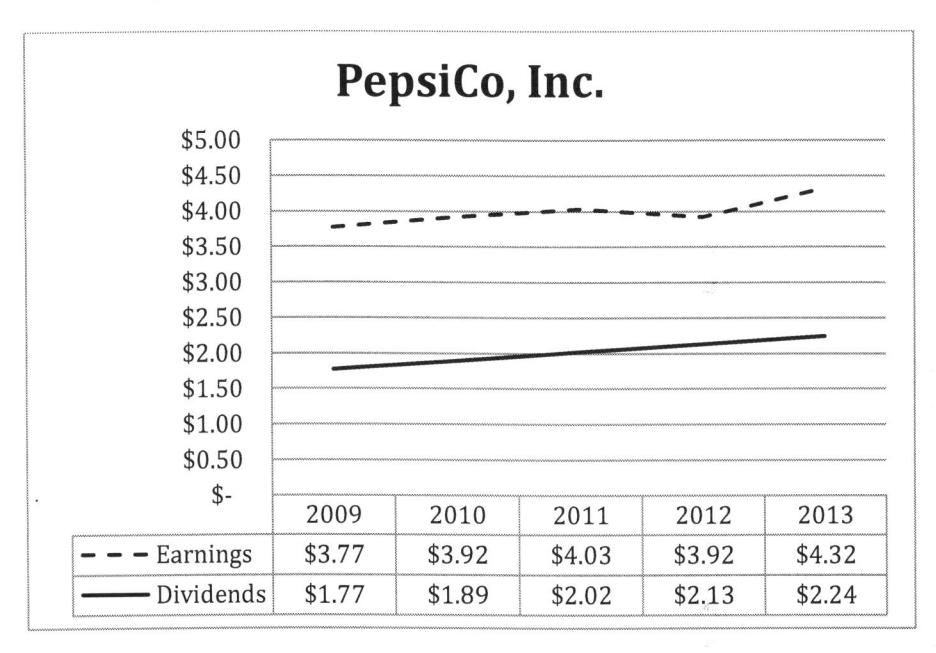

PepsiCo, Inc.

	2009	2010	2011	2012	2013
Earnings	$3.77	$3.92	$4.03	$3.92	$4.32
Dividends	$1.77	$1.89	$2.02	$2.13	$2.24

PepsiCo's management is determined to grow dividends at a faster rate going forward. If you invest $10,000 in PepsiCo in 2014, your current yield will be about 3.2 percent. In 2019, your holdings will have a yield on cost of 5.2 percent, and your annual dividend payments will have increased to $515. After 20 years, your annual dividend payment will be $2,820.

The soda wars will continue for years to come, but PepsiCo and Coke will continue to be successful. As consumers' taste preferences change, both PepsiCo and Coke will change with them. Both companies will continue to acquire brands they think will be successful in their respective portfolios. Dividend growth investors will be rewarded for buying and holding PepsiCo and Coke.

Chapter 11

Potash Corp. of Saskatchewan

Potash Corporation of Saskatchewan Inc. (Ticker: POT) is an integrated fertilizer and industrial and feed products company. It's the worlds largest fertilizer company by capacity. The company operates in three segments: potash, phosphate and nitrogen. These three business segments serve as a stabilizer for the volatile price swings of each segment's underlying commodity. The company owns and operates five potash mines in Saskatchewan and one in New Brunswick. It has operations in seven countries including China. Its phosphate operations include the production and sale of liquid and solid phosphate fertilizers, phosphate feed and industrial acid, which is used in food products and industrial processes. Potash has a phosphate mine and two mineral processing plants in Florida and five phosphates feed plants in other parts of the country. In Louisiana, the company produces phosphoric acid.

Potash was hit hard in the middle of 2013 due to a shake up in the supply and demand dynamics. The Russian potash-producing firm, Uralkali, decided to withdraw from the Russo-Belarusian potash cartel BPC. This essentially broke up the cartel and allowed for prices to drop. It's analogous to Saudi Arabia leaving the Organization of the Petroleum Exporting Countries (OPEC) and selling its oil at a lower price than OPEC designates. Oil prices would drop dramatically as barrels of oil are sold below OPEC's target level. Oil companies' profit margins would shrink or disappear for a time until economic conditions changed.

Potash Corp. dropped by 30 percent because it holds the largest amount of potash in the world and it's the company's primary revenue source. Was this sell-off justified? After all, the company is still very profitable and long-term phosphate demand is still intact, but the stock price declined too much to be justified by the potash demand issue. There was panic selling by mutual funds and retail investors. No one wanted to own a big loser so everyone sold. There was very little demand for this stock during the second half of 2013. In 2014, Potash Corp. trades at a price to earnings ratio of 14. This is a very reasonable valuation to purchase your first shares.

Dividend growth has been off the charts in the last few years. Potash's trailing five-year dividend growth rate is 79 percent. This is due to a few different reasons: the company started with a small dividend, extraordinary growth happened during those five years, and management is dividend-growth oriented. Going forward, the dividend growth rate will slow considerably to between 12 – 15 percent. For our dividend forecast model, we'll use the more conservative growth rate of 12 percent.

Potash Corp's management is bringing the company into a mature dividend growth phase. If you invested $10,000 in Potash in 2009, your investment would be worth $11,875 in 2013. Dividends paid during that five-year period were $918. The majority of dividend payments came in 2012 and 2013. The compounded annual growth rate of your investment would have been 6.3 percent.

Potash Corp

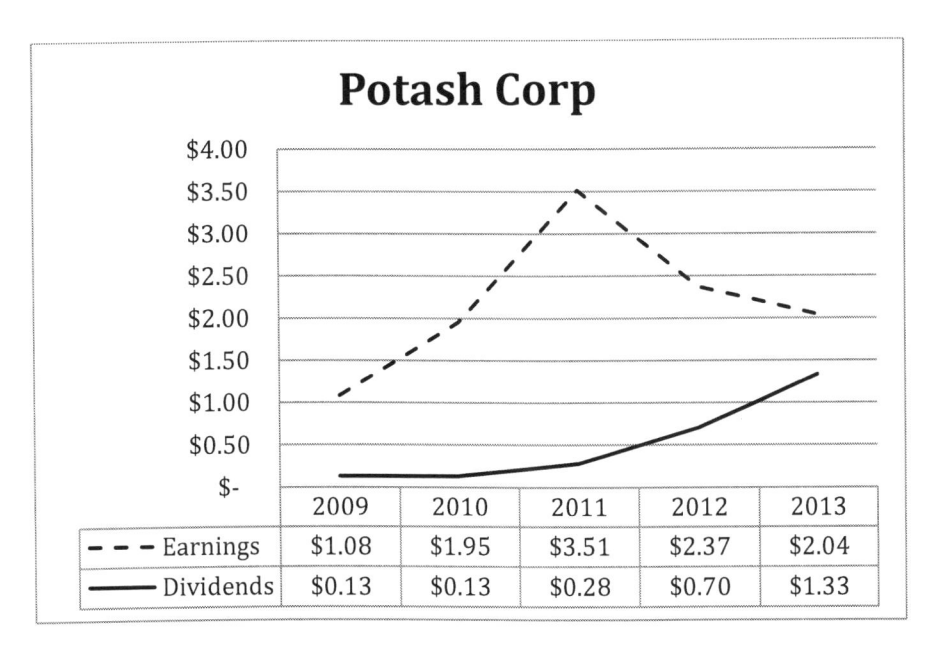

	2009	2010	2011	2012	2013
- - - Earnings	$1.08	$1.95	$3.51	$2.37	$2.04
—— Dividends	$0.13	$0.13	$0.28	$0.70	$1.33

If you invest $10,000 in Potash Corp. in 2014, you can expect to receive a current dividend yield of about 4 percent or $1.40 per share. This translates into an annual dividend payment of $425. If management can grow dividends by 12 percent per year, your annual dividend payment will increase to $748 in 2019. After 20 years, you can expect an annual dividend payment of $4,100.

There will be a demand for potash in the future like the world has never seen in the past. With more people around the globe moving into the middle class, more food will be needed. One of the best ways to produce more food is with fertilizer (potash, phosphate, and nitrogen). There is only a certain amount of arable land in the world. Farmers will need to produce more food with the same amount of land. Food density per acre has been increasing for years, and the trend is that it will continue.

Barriers to entry in the fertilizer market are extremely high, with limited deposits of potash worldwide. There are multi-billion-dollar development costs and time investments upward of seven years. Global producers can only produce a certain amount of potash; their capacity is limited. When global demand increases during the next few years, Potash Corp. stands in a unique position to deliver potash at very profitable prices.

Chapter 12

ConocoPhillips

ConocoPhillips (Ticker: COP) explores and produces crude oil, natural gas, natural gas liquids, liquefied natural gas and bitumen around the world. The company is headquartered out of Houston, Texas and operates in North America, Europe, Asia, and Australia. ConocoPhillips is the largest independent exploration and production (E&P) oil company in the world. Exploration and production is also known as "upstream" oil production, because it's the first process in the production of oil and its eventual refinement to various fuels.

Exploration and production companies are usually known for their high risk/high reward profile; however, ConocoPhillips doesn't fit the normal profile of an E&P company. The company has many existing operations in place when it comes to production, so the risky side of the business is the exploration, which makes up a relatively small percentage of Conoco's operations. Any sunk costs related to exploration are easily covered by the company's production business.

Revenues and earnings have not gone straight up from 2009 to 2013; however, earnings per share have gone up every year due to share buybacks. The company has been buying back shares since 2009, from 1.5 billion shares outstanding in 2009 to 1.24 billion shares outstanding at the end of 2013. This means that about 250 million shares at about $60 per share on average have been repurchased! This increases the value of every share that you own. Like any commodity related company, this company's revenue and earnings will fluctuate with the price of oil, but management's commitment to share buybacks has lifted earnings per share since 2009.

ConocoPhillips' goal is to give shareholders a consistent and reliable return on their investment through steadily growing dividends and increasing earnings per share. The company achieves this through intelligent capital allocation, share repurchases, and increasing the payments it makes to shareholders. Although the company did not raise its dividend from 2011 to 2012, management is now focused on raising the dividend again.

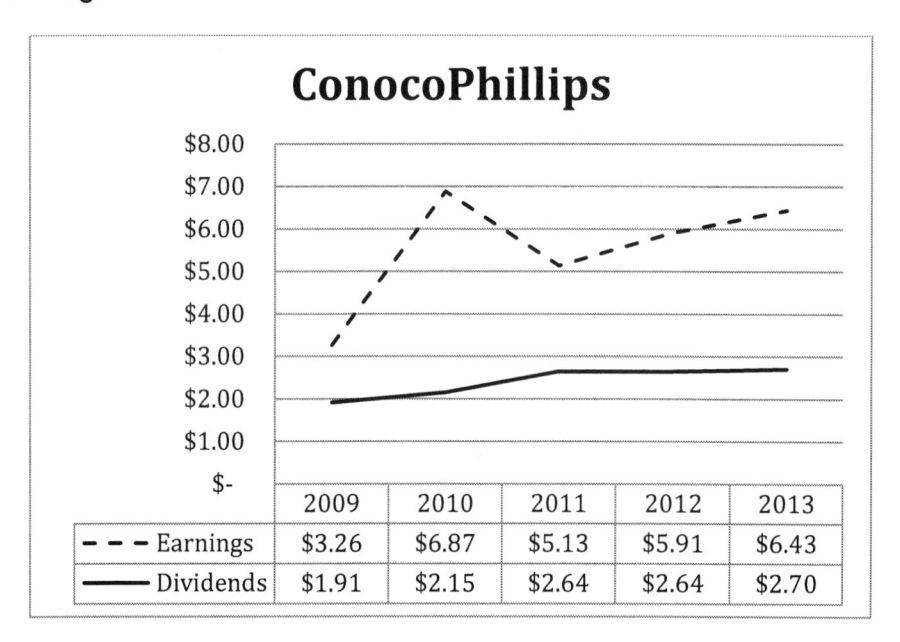

ConocoPhillips

	2009	2010	2011	2012	2013
Earnings	$3.26	$6.87	$5.13	$5.91	$6.43
Dividends	$1.91	$2.15	$2.64	$2.64	$2.70

During the past five years, Conoco Philip's dividend has gone from $1.91 to $2.70 annually. This translates into a five-year compound annual growth rate of 9 percent. That 9 percent growth rate will be used for the forecasted dividends. If you invest $10,000 in COP in 2014, you can expect to receive an annual dividend of about $420. If this investment is held until 2019, it will produce an annual dividend payment of about $650. In 2034, COP will produce $2,350 in annual dividend payments.

Chapter 13

Altria Group, Inc.

Altria Group, Inc., (Ticker: MO) manufactures and sells tobacco products in the United States. It is the parent company of the following: Phillip Morris USA Inc., John Middleton Co., UST LLC, and PM Capital Corporation. Altria Group, Inc. Altria Group also owns 26.9 percent of SABMiller plc, a multinational brewing and beverage company headquartered in London. Altria owns brands such as Marlboro, Copenhagen, Skoal, and Black & Mild.

Altria Group is basically the domestic version of Phillip Morris International (see Chapter 3). The difference is that Altria operates solely in the United States so is limited to the lower growth potential of the U.S. Altria is expected to grow more slowly than Phillip Morris; however, the slower growth rate doesn't mean the company isn't investable. To the contrary – Altria has been one of the all-time best performers in the S&P 500 and deserves your hard earned capital.

Altria Group's dividend payout ratio is high compared to many other dividend paying stocks. In 2009, the company changed its target dividend payout ratio from approximately 75 to 80 percent of earnings. The fiscal year ending on December 31, 2013 saw a dividend payout ratio of 81 percent. Management was successful in keeping the dividend payout ratio at the targeted range. This is important because it shows that management is meeting its goals and the company is performing in-line with expectations.

Altria Group, Inc.

	2009	2010	2011	2012	2013
– – – Earnings	$1.54	$1.87	$1.64	$2.06	$2.27
——— Dividends	$1.32	$1.46	$1.58	$1.70	$1.84

Altria's total shareholder return for the five years ending December 31, 2013, was 244.7 percent. A $10,000 investment during this time would have turned into $24,470. Your annual dividend payment in 2014 would be $1,200. The company is committed to increasing returns to shareholders. Altria has increased its dividend 47 times in the last 45 years. The company has achieved an annualized dividend growth rate of 8.5 percent from 2009 to the end of 2013. In the future, you can expect Altria to raise its dividend by 7 to 11 percent every year.

For our projections, we'll use a compound dividend growth rate of 10 percent annually. Altria generated free cash flow of $5.5 billion in 2013, while it paid out only $3.6 billion in dividends during the year. Although the payout ratio is quite high, Altria will be able to continue to raise its dividend based on earnings growth and share repurchases. There is a margin of safety in this stock that will keep it from going under $30 per share. The high dividend puts a floor on the stock price; investors will bid the stock up if the dividend yield goes too high (over 6 percent range)

If you invest $10,000 into Altria in 2014, your dividend payment will be about $550 (current dividend yield is 5.5 percent). After holding your investment for five years, your annual dividend payment will be about $885 in 2019. After a twenty-year holding period, your annual dividend payment will be about $3,700.

There is little downside to this stock at its current price level of mid-thirties at the time of this writing. The stock will sell off in a recession, although not as much as a high-flying, high-beta social media stock. People will continue to smoke in the United States into the foreseeable future. As they quit smoking traditional cigarettes, some consumers will transition into using electronic cigarettes.

The electronic cigarette revolution is in place and Altria Group is finally on board with a product. The company introduced its MarkTen brand electronic cigarette in February of 2014. It's too early to get the results for MarkTen, so financial forecasts cannot be updated to reflect the new technology. MarkTen was first introduced in Indiana and Arizona. The great news for Altria is that it was able to capture 48 percent of the electronic cigarette market share in Arizona within two months.

Altria also acquired Green Smoke, another electronic cigarette maker that has over 3.5 million users. Green Smoke is the premium brand electronic cigarette that could have the potential to be the Marlboro of electronic cigarettes. It may have been part of Altria's strategy to see which electronic cigarette brand would capture a large market share and then acquire it. This way the company avoids development costs and other sunk costs that would have been lost had their own product not gained traction.

Chapter 14

Kinder Morgan Partners, L.P.

Kinder Morgan Partner, L.P. (Ticker: KMP) is a master limited partnership that is involved with midstream oil operations. With approximately 47,000 miles, this company has more miles of pipeline in America than any other operator. The partnership's general partner is Kinder Morgan, Inc. (KMI), and if you become a unit-holder in the partnership, you are said to be a Limited Partner. The partnership has rewarded unit-holders with a compound annual growth rate of 24 percent since 1997, the year the partnership started. The combined Kinder Morgan companies make up the largest midstream operator and the third largest energy company in America, at over $100 billion enterprise value.

Investing in master limited partnerships can be complicated, but doesn't have to be. Owners of limited partnership units receive a K-1 tax form in late January or early February of each year. This form shows distributions that the individual investor receives. It also shows how much of this distribution is considered a return of capital. Return of capital is typically not taxable. The only way it is taxed is if your cost basis goes below zero. Going below zero on the tax basis for Master Limited Partnerships (MLPs) takes many years; that's why MLPs are such a great investment in a taxable account.

MLPs should always be placed in taxable accounts because the "dividends" you receive are mostly considered a return of capital and are not taxable. Placing them in a retirement account is allowed but would make little sense given they're already tax favored. If you invest in $100 worth of a master limited partnership, you may receive about $7 in "dividends" during your first year [note: these "dividends" are actually distributions, so technically it's not a dividend]. When you receive your K-1 for the respective tax year, you'll see that your cost basis will now be about $93, your return of capital close to $7, and a very small amount will be taxable. The great thing is that you don't have to pay tax on the $7, and you can then reinvest back into the MLP or allocate it to a different investment. When your cost basis in a master limited partnership falls below zero, the distributions are then taxed as ordinary income.

In early 2014, Kinder Morgan Partners decreased to about $75 per share, or just over 6 percent. This discount in share price was primarily caused by a Barron's article claiming that Kinder was not properly accounting for replacement and upgrading costs properly. Barron's warned that the company is going to need more cash than they set aside for capital expenditures. This, of course, is not a new allegation. There was also an article in late 2013 that claimed the same thing but didn't gain traction.

Barron's came out with a similar piece about Linn Energy (LINE, LNCO) in 2013, which caused a sharp drop in Linn's stock price. Linn's situation was quite different than that of Kinder's. Linn's issue was mostly due to their accounting of put contracts. Linn Energy is coming through the allegations and continuing to increase distributions to unit-holders. Their stock price has recovered by about 50 percent off the lows.

Kinder Morgan Partners price per share is very attractive in 2014, and now is a perfect time to buy units. The current "dividend" yield is very high at over seven percent, and the distribution growth rate is likely to exceed five percent per year in perpetuity. If you purchase $10,000 worth of Kinder (KMP) in 2014, your first annual dividend payments will equal $725. At a 6 percent "dividend" growth rate, your annual payments will be over $1000 in 2019 and $2400 in 2034.

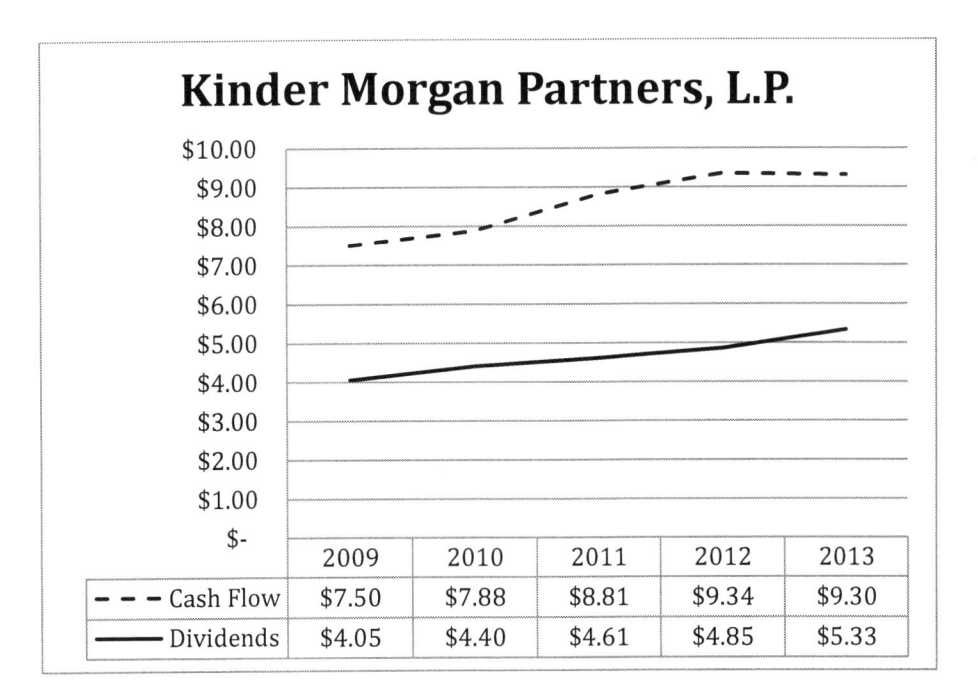

Kinder Morgan Partners, L.P.

	2009	2010	2011	2012	2013
– – – Cash Flow	$7.50	$7.88	$8.81	$9.34	$9.30
—— Dividends	$4.05	$4.40	$4.61	$4.85	$5.33

Chapter 15

Enterprise Products Partners, L.P.

Enterprise Products Partners, L.P. (Ticker: EPD) is a master limited partnership that is involved with midstream oil operations, much like Kinder Morgan Partners, L.P. Enterprise is one of the best partnerships you can buy on the market today. They are a North American provider of midstream services to producers of natural gas, natural gas liquids (NGLs), crude oil, and petrochemicals. The company has five business segments: Onshore natural gas pipelines & services, onshore crude oil pipelines & services, natural gas liquid pipelines and services, offshore pipelines & services, and petrochemical & refined products services.

Enterprise has huge growth prospects for 2014 and beyond. They have projects worth $5 billion in 2014. The Appalachia-to-Texas (ATEX) Express Pipeline will come on line to take natural gas from Pennsylvania, Ohio, and West Virginia down to the Gulf Coast. This will provide extra fee-based revenue that will increase operating margins.

EPD is a big player in the midstream natural gas market, and the rise in natural gas prices will help with margins. The companies that pay Enterprise to pipe its product to refineries are more likely to pay premium prices to have their products piped because of higher natural gas prices. As long as demand for natural gas is strong, this company will continue to achieve high margins.

Enterprise's has historically had a lower current "dividend" yield than Kinder Morgan's yield. Enterprise has potentially better growth prospects, especially beginning 2014 through 2016. Enterprise has a current yield of about 4.2 percent, which is relatively low for a master limited partnership. You can expect the yield to rise quite a bit over the next few years as Enterprise wraps up construction on several pipelines. The relatively low yield will increase by 8-10 percent over the next five years.

With a 10 percent "dividend" growth rate and a current yield of about 4.2 percent, Enterprise will make a great addition to your portfolio. Cash flow will increase in 2014 due to the commencement of pipelines like the ATEX. The low current yield will allow Enterprise to grow its distribution rate at a greater rate than its peers.

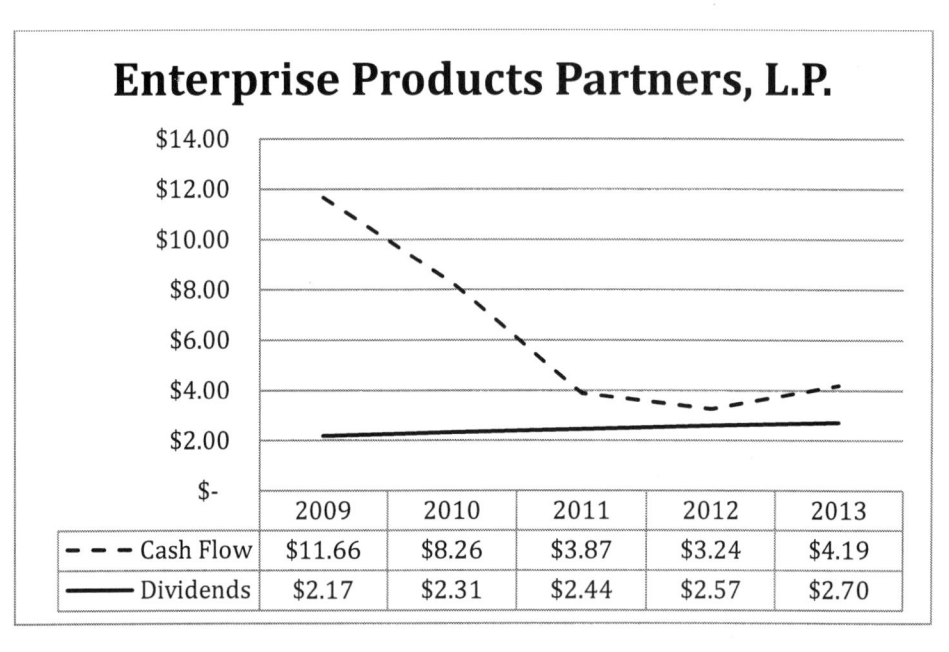

Enterprise Products Partners, L.P.

	2009	2010	2011	2012	2013
− − − Cash Flow	$11.66	$8.26	$3.87	$3.24	$4.19
——— Dividends	$2.17	$2.31	$2.44	$2.57	$2.70

A $10,000 investment into Enterprise Products Partners, L.P. in 2014 will produce $420 in annual distributions. At 10 percent growth, annual distributions will be $725 in 2019 and $3,025 in 2034. The potential for Enterprise is even greater than 10 percent annual growth in distributions. The company holds key pipelines that will enable it to increase fee-based revenue. Their margins will expand nicely with an increase in fee-based revenue.

Chapter 16

Kinder Morgan, Inc.

Kinder Morgan, Inc. (Ticker: KMI) is the incorporated business structure of the Kinder Morgan portfolio of companies. It is not a master limited partnership and as such does not offer the tax shelter that MLPs do. It derives most of its income from Kinder Morgan Partners, L.P. (KMP) and El Paso Pipeline Partners (EPB). The reason Kinder Morgan, Inc. was formed in 2011 was to offer investors a way to invest into Kinder without the complications of partnerships and their tax structure. Think of Kinder Morgan, Inc. as the dealmaker. It's the place where all the deals happen, but none of the oil business is transacted through it. KMI is the general partner in master limited partnerships.

Since Kinder Morgan, Inc. (KMI) is set up as a corporation, investors should own shares through a tax-shelter vehicle like an IRA if possible. KMI has a relatively high current yield at over 5 percent. Having KMI's dividends sheltered from current taxes will allow you to reinvest one hundred percent of them. KMI has only been around since 2011, but is committed to raising dividends several times per year.

In 2012, KMI paid an annual dividend of $1.34. KMI then raised their total annual dividend to $1.56, an astonishing growth rate of 16.4 percent. This growth rate will not continue permanently, but the dividend growth investor should expect a high growth rate in the next several years, ultimately slowing to a 5 to 6 percent long-term growth rate. Given that this company has only been trading since 2011, the following graph will show future dividend payments of KMI.

Kinder Morgan, Inc. Forecasted Dividends

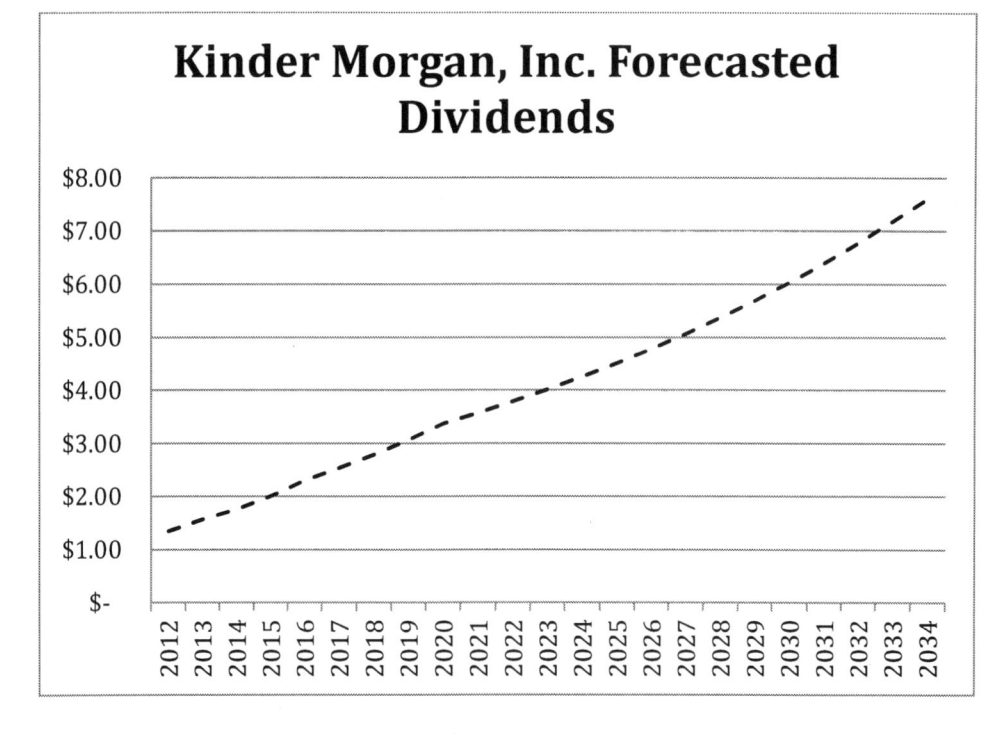

Kinder Morgan Partners, L.P (KMP), will primarily drive the company's dividends. $10,000 invested in KMI in 2014 will produce an annual dividend payment of $550. If this investment is held until 2019, it will produce an annual dividend payment of about $950. In 2034, KMI will produce over $2400 in annual dividend payments.

      Investing into the incorporated class of shares is a great way to ride the coattails of legendary businessman, Richard Kinder. Mr. Kinder turned a micro-cap company into the third largest energy company in North America. There is a popular saying that you should invest in people, not companies. That statement couldn't be more accurate when it comes to Richard Kinder. He is the Jeff Bezos of energy companies. As long as Richard is running the company, you can be sure to receive a great return on your investment.

      In early 2014, Kinder Morgan, Inc. (KMI) went on sale because of a hit piece by Barron's (a weekly periodical that your author reads). Barron's wants to attract eyeballs so that they can sell advertising and expand readership. The piece on Kinder (search Google for "Kinder Morgan: Trouble in the Pipelines?") was unoriginal and ill advised. Journalists, even if they have a financial background, know very little about individual companies. They generally know very little about anything, except for writing thousand word articles on topics that will get attention. This is great for the patient dividend growth investor. When fearful investors discount stocks, dividend growth investors can purchase shares and receive a higher current yield and a higher margin of safety.

Chapter 17

Kimberly Clark Corp

Kimberly Clark Corp. (Ticker: KMB) manufactures and markets branded products globally. The company's brands include Huggies, Kleenex, Kotex, Scott's and many others. The company operates in four business segments: Personal Care, Consumer Tissue, K-C Professional, and Health Care. The company is a true multi-national corporation with a heavy focus on selling products in China, Russia, and Latin America.

The company is committed to returning value to shareholders in the form of stock buybacks and increasing dividends. It has maintained a consistent stock buyback program in the past. Between 2003 and 2013, the number of shares decreased from 509 million to 385 million, or about a quarter of the entire company. Dividends have increased from $2.40 in 2009 to $3.24 in 2013, a five-year compound annual growth rate of 7.8 percent.

Kimberly-Clark's North American unit has been a weak performer in the past; however, the "Focused On Reducing Costs Everywhere" program, or FORCE for short, has been highly successful. This cost-cutting program saved the company $310 million in 2013 through the closing of facilities and elimination of positions. It is estimated that the FORCE program will save the company over $300 million in 2014. This is especially important because of the recent inflation in inputs the company has faced. Importantly, this inflation has been offset by the reduction in expenses within the FORCE program. The company has been able to increase their gross profit margin from the prior period in each of the last three years, 2011, 2012, and 2013. This is directly related to the successful FORCE program.

Kimberly-Clark has a long-term Global Business Plan that identifies their financial goals. The company's plan calls for sales growth between 3 to 5 percent, earnings per share growth in the high single digits, and dividend growth in line with earnings' growth. As a dividend growth investor, we prefer a dividend growth rate of ten percent or greater, but even though the company's dividend growth rate is below eight percent, it's still a buy since it has great global growth prospects and is a defensive stock.

People will continue to buy Huggies diapers and Scott's tissue paper, even in a recession. There is a risk that during a recession, consumers will switch to less expensive private labels. This risk is low though since Kimberly-Clark has a top-notch marketing department. It is likely that the company would discount their products and offer more generous coupons in a recession. Their margins will be squeezed in a recession; however, this squeeze will only be temporary. Over the long-term, you can expect Kimberly-Clark to expand margins driven by their overseas sales and cost-cutting efforts. As consumers' disposable incomes in developing countries climb, they're more likely to buy branded products. This will drive sales and margin expansion at Kimberly-Clark for years to come.

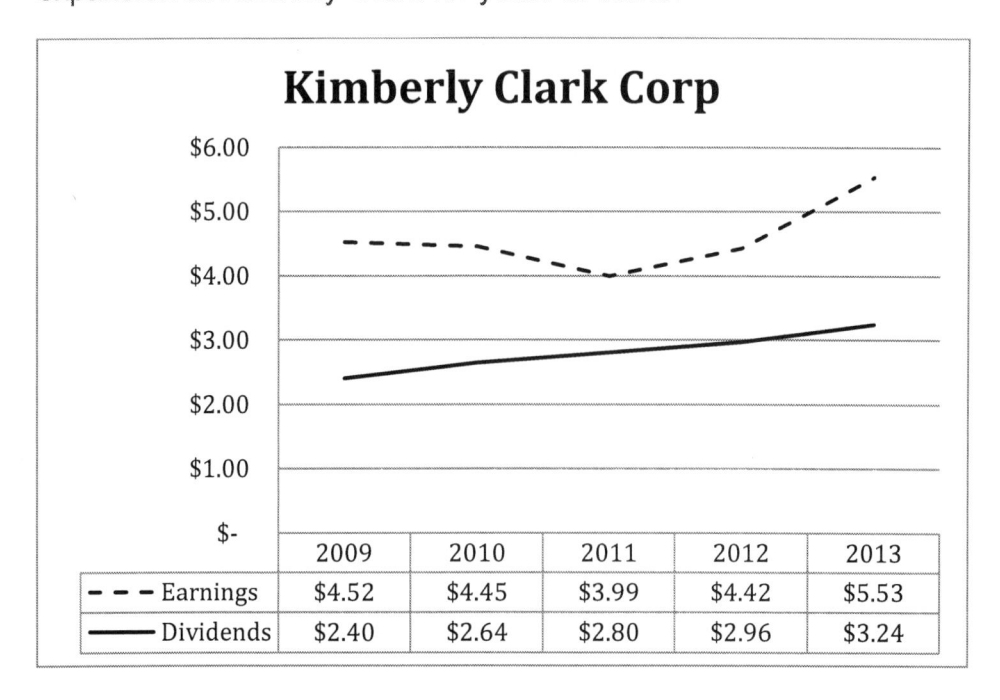

Kimberly Clark Corp

	2009	2010	2011	2012	2013
- - - Earnings	$4.52	$4.45	$3.99	$4.42	$5.53
—— Dividends	$2.40	$2.64	$2.80	$2.96	$3.24

During the past five years, Kimberly-Clark's dividend has gone from $2.40 to $3.24 annually. This translates into a five-year compound annual growth rate of 7.8 percent. The company is firing on all cylinders with their cost-cutting efforts and overseas expansion. Going forward, KMB's dividend growth rate will be about 10 percent. If you invest $10,000 in KMB in 2014, you can expect to receive an annual dividend of about $330. If this investment is held until 2019, it will produce an annual dividend payment of about $870. In 2034, KMB will produce over $2,500 in annual dividend payments.

Chapter 18

Procter & Gamble, Inc.

Procter & Gamble, Inc. (Ticker: PG) is a multi-national manufacturer of branded household products. P&G products are sold in almost every country in the world. Its brands include Tide, Charmin, Gillette, Pampers, Cascade, Dawn, Olay and many others. P&G has the some of the world's most recognizable brands, and many of their brands are number one in their respective categories. The company operates in five different business segments: Beauty; Grooming; Health Care; Home Care and Fabric Care; and Baby Care and Family Care.

The company's brands sell large volumes and have very good profits. Procter & Gamble's top 50 brands account for 90 percent of sales and profits. The top 25 brands each bring in at least $1 billion in revenue annually. In fiscal year 2013, P&G had revenues of $84 billion and profits of $11.3 billion.

The increase in revenue is small, with year over year growth of just a half a percent from 2012 to 2013. One of the challenges that face Procter and Gamble is that its revenue growth is almost non-existent. This is primarily because P&G has saturated the market with many of their brands. They're sales are so large, that a billion dollar increase in sales would only account for just over one percent of total sales. It's the rule of large numbers. It's much easier to double sales if a company generates a few million in revenues each year. When a company has $80 billion of sales, it's nearly impossible to double sales.

Procter & Gamble is able to increase earnings per share because of the smaller outstanding share count each year. The company buys back shares in its own stock on a regular basis, thus making each share a bigger part of the total equity pie. This shrinking of the company is the main reason why earnings per share will grow going forward.

Procter & Gamble

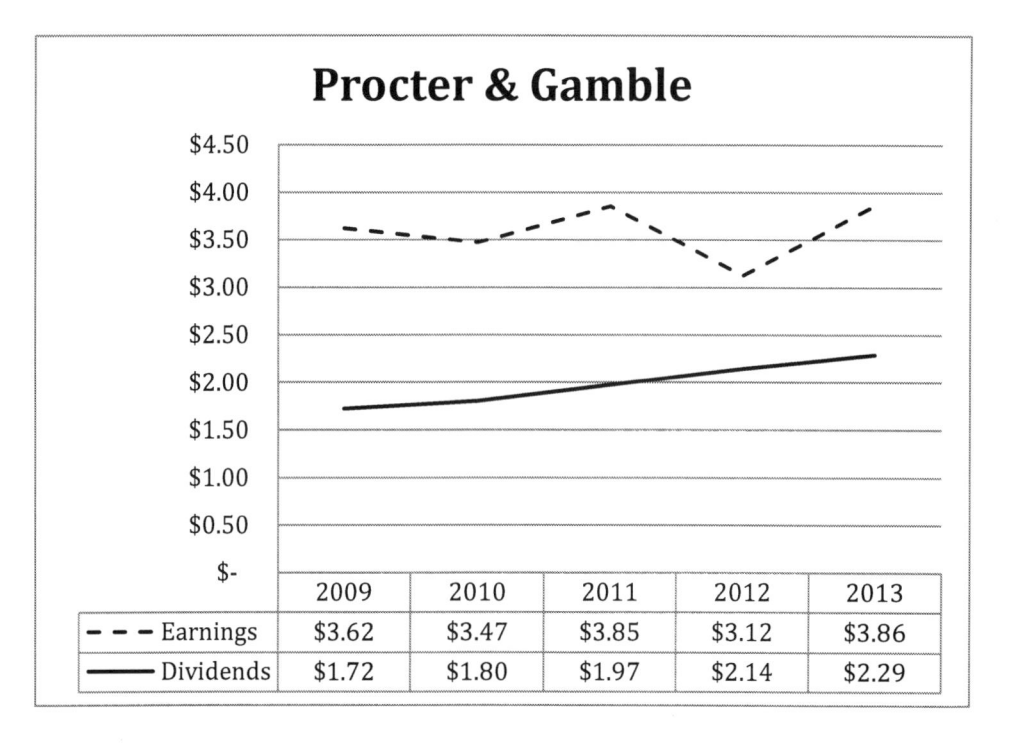

	2009	2010	2011	2012	2013
− − − Earnings	$3.62	$3.47	$3.85	$3.12	$3.86
—— Dividends	$1.72	$1.80	$1.97	$2.14	$2.29

Share buybacks combined with overseas growth make this stock a must own for every dividend investor. The company has a relatively small dividend yield of just over 3 percent. The five-year dividend growth rate from 2009 to 2013 was 7.4 percent. Going forward, the annual dividend growth rate should be closer to 9 percent. This will be primarily due to the share buyback program.

If you invest $10,000 in P&G in 2014, you can expect to receive an annual dividend of about $310. If this investment is held until 2019, it will produce an annual dividend payment of about $480. In 2034, P&G will produce over $1,750 in annual dividend payments.

Procter & Gamble's stock is a very reliable and conservative investment. Investors who want faster growth in the same sector, non-cyclical consumer goods and services, should invest in Kimberly-Clark before Procter & Gamble. P&G's beta is 0.42, one of the lowest of all the stocks recommended in this book. During a recession, P&G will outperform almost all other stocks in the S&P 500. This is because P&G is a non-cyclical company with some of the best-known brands in the world.

Investing in P&G's stock at the right price is essential for getting the most dividends for your principle invested. Buy this stock below a trailing-twelve-month price to earnings ratio of 20. This will give you a margin of safety and a decent current dividend yield.

Chapter 19

Johnson & Johnson

"Being global is something you can't do vicariously."

~Alex Gorsky, CEO of Johnson & Johnson

Johnson & Johnson (Ticker: JNJ) is a diversified healthcare company with brands like Tylenol, Visine, Splenda, and Listerine. The company also has a medical devices and diagnostics business that sells products most consumers have never heard of like Cordis Cardiology, Topamax, Levaquin, and Xerelto. Cordis makes stents for patients with coronary artery disease, and Topamax, Levaquin, and Xerelto are a full line of prescription drugs produced by Johnson & Johnson.

Johnson & Johnson's major competitors include Pfizer (PFE), Bristol Myers Squibb (BMY) and Novartis (NVS). Although there are many healthcare companies for a dividend investor to choose from, JNJ has broadest diversification of revenues. It sells products across many product lines, not just prescription drugs.

Johnson & Johnson stock generated an 8.9 percent total return for investors from 2003 to 2013. In comparison, the S&P 500 generated a 7.4 percent total return. This shows that the company can outperform the S&P 500 index, even though it's a mature, relatively slow-growing company. It is able to achieve this because of the company's superior management team.

Alex Gorsky is the CEO and Chairman of the Board for Johnson & Johnson. With his leadership, the company is performing better than its peers and will continue to do so. Gorsky took over as CEO in 2012 and is likely to lead the company for at least a decade. JNJ doesn't change CEOs often, with only 8 leaders in their 126-year history. Gorsky isn't expected shake things up at Johnson & Johnson. The company already has a long and successful track record as a top performer.

What you can expect out of the new CEO is that he will drive higher sales by sharpening execution of Johnson & Johnson's pharmaceutical business. Gorsky is first and foremost a highly successful salesman. Recently, the company has had issues with some of their pharmaceutical products. In 2013, the company had to recall one lot of Risperdal Consta, an injectable antipsychotic treatment. Mold was found in the drug repeatedly. That was the last of Johnson & Johnson's major recalls after years of struggling with different issue. Gorsky has led the company to have few recalls. In 2014, the company hasn't had any major recalls of their pharmaceutical products.

Johnson & Johnson is a mega-cap company with a small but steady dividend growth rate. During the five-year period from 2009 to 2013, JNJ raised its annual dividend from $1.93 to $2.59. The company's five-year dividend growth rate is 7.6 percent. With Alex Gorsky at the helm and good pharmaceutical business going forward, you can expect a 9 percent dividend growth rate.

Johnson & Johnson

	2009	2010	2011	2012	2013
– – – Earnings	$4.40	$4.78	$3.49	$3.86	$4.81
—— Dividends	$1.93	$2.11	$2.25	$2.40	$2.59

If you invest $10,000 in Johnson & Johnson in 2014, you can expect an annual dividend payment of $286. In 2019, the annual dividend payment will grow to $440. After holding JNJ for 20 years, in 2034 the annual dividend payment will grow to $1,600. Johnson & Johnson is a slow and steady dividend grower. It's a very safe investment with a very nice risk to reward ratio. It's almost like holding a bond with a 3 percent yield, but has the advantage of a stock. Its earnings will increase substantially in the years to come, and the stock price will follow.

Chapter 20

The Clorox Company

The Clorox Company (Ticker: CLX) is a manufacturer and marketer of professional and consumer products. Clorox operates in four business segments: Cleaning, Household, Lifestyle and International. The Clorox portfolio of brands includes many first and second ranked brands in their respective categories. The brands Clorox owns are: Hidden Valley, Burt's Bees, Formula 409, Green Works, Pine-Sol, Kingsford, Brita, Fresh Step, Scoop Away, and many others. The company acquired Soy Vay Enterprises, Inc., HealthLink, Aplicare, Inc. in fiscal year 2012.

Clorox has a long-term strategic plan called Vision 2020. The company plans to grow net sales by 3 to 5 percent annually, expand earnings before interest and income taxes (EBIT) margin 25 to 50 basis points annually, and generate free cash flow of 10 to 12 percent of sales annually. The 2020 Strategy includes four ways to achieve the above metrics:

1. *Engage our people as business owners.*
2. *Increase our brand investment behind superior products and more targeted 3D plans.*
3. *Grow into profitable new categories, channels and countries.*
4. *Fund growth by reducing waste in our work, products and supply chain.*

If you invest $10,000 in Clorox in 2014, you can expect an annual dividend payment of $322. For our forecast, we use a 10 percent annual dividend growth rate. In 2019, the annual dividend payment will grow to $520. After holding CLX for 20 years, in 2034 the annual dividend payment will grow to $2,170.

Clorox Co

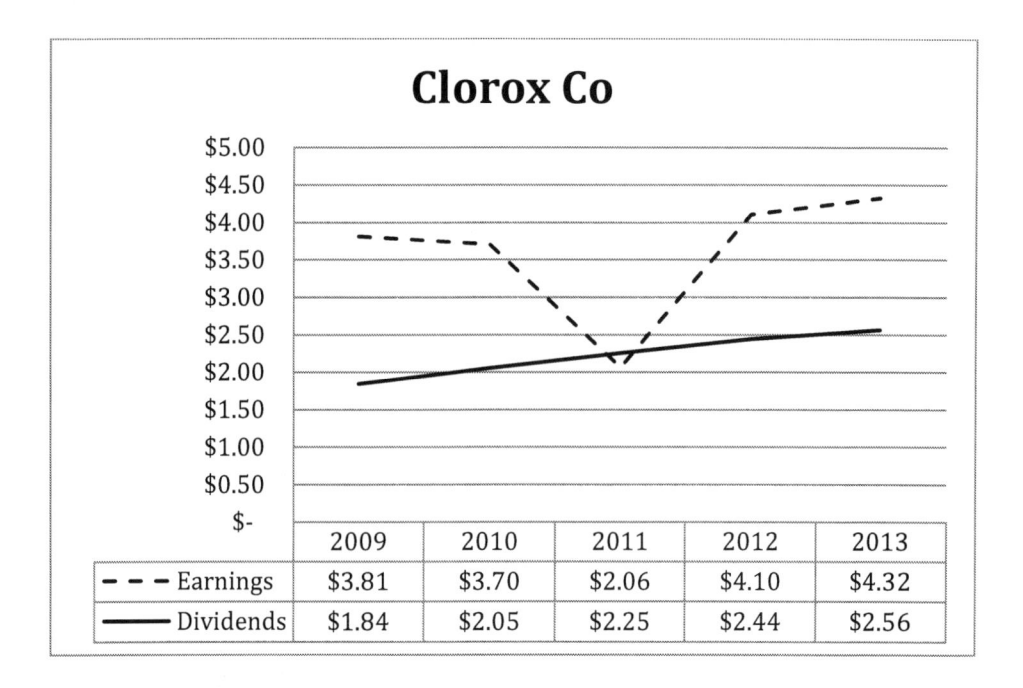

	2009	2010	2011	2012	2013
- - - Earnings	$3.81	$3.70	$2.06	$4.10	$4.32
——— Dividends	$1.84	$2.05	$2.25	$2.44	$2.56

Clorox' growth in earnings and dividends make it a great investment for the dividend growth investor. Over the past five years, Clorox has grown its dividend by 8.5 percent per year. Going forward, Clorox should be able to grow dividends at 10 percent annually.

Chapter 21

AT&T

AT&T (Ticker: T) is a provider of telecommunications services, which consists of wireless communications, local exchange services, long-distance services, internet services, video services, and equipment. The company operates in three business segments: Wireless, Wireline, and Other. The Other business segment includes operator services and corporate operations. In March 2014, AT&T acquired the prepaid wireless provider Leap Wireless International.

The wireless market is highly competitive and faces downward pricing pressures; however, AT&T has shown that it is nimble enough to stay highly competitive and profitable. During 2013, T-Mobile and other wireless carriers fought viciously to gain new customers. T-Mobile specifically went after AT&T's customer base during this battle. T-Mobile paid AT&T's customers to switch to their network. In an effort to keep its own customers from leaving, AT&T slashed its prices in February 2014. T-Mobile's efforts in 2013 didn't harm AT&T's total wireless subscriber count, at about 72.6 million by the end of 2013. AT&T's wireless customer count continues to grow every year. They control about 33 percent of the market, behind Verizon Wireless at 35 percent. AT&T's profit was $18.2 billion in 2013, clearly showing that the company has no sign of profit margin erosion from pricing pressures in the wireless market.

AT&T has plenty of room to grow and should take market share from other carriers. Even though AT&T has a hefty 72.6 million subscribers, they have room to expand that to well over 100 million subscribers in the years to come. Population growth will account for some subscriber growth. As millennials join the workforce, they're more likely to drop off of their parents plan. There are 31.4 million people ages 18 to 24. Assuming that about 33 percent of those 18-24 year olds join AT&T's wireless network over the next few years, you get about 10.4 million new subscribers. This level of growth is great for a mature company.

AT&T pays a high current yield of over 5 percent, but has a very low dividend growth rate. Over the past five years, AT&T has managed to grow its dividends at annual compound growth rate of 2.7 percent. This rate of dividend growth is very small, and a good dividend growth investor would be hesitant to buy a stock with such a low dividend growth rate.

In this case, AT&T is a buy because of its high current dividend yield and its potential for higher future growth in dividends. AT&T should grow its dividend by about 5 percent going forward. This will be caused by growth in wireless subscribers, and huge growth in data plans. AT&T is a cash machine that you have to have in your portfolio.

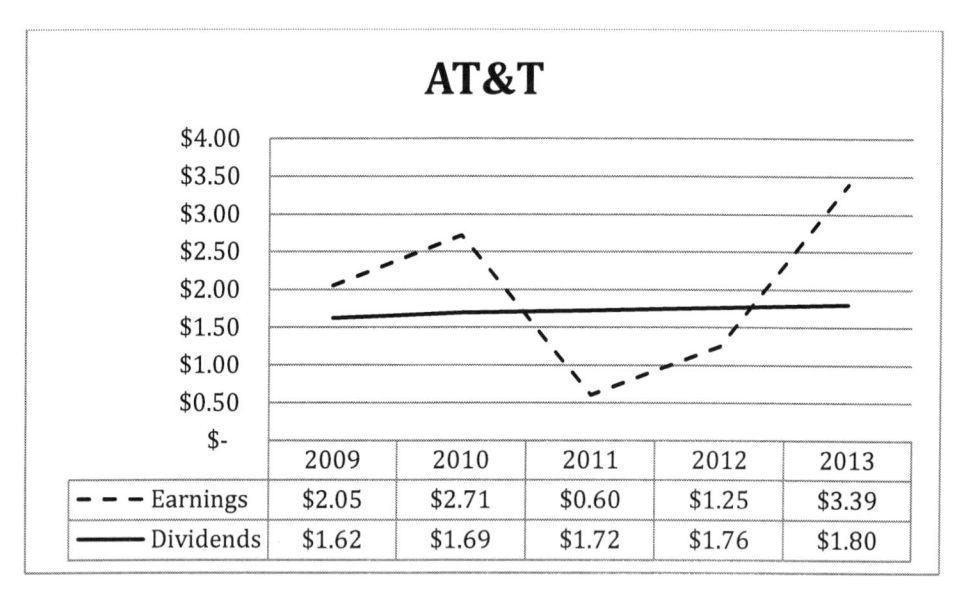

AT&T

	2009	2010	2011	2012	2013
--- Earnings	$2.05	$2.71	$0.60	$1.25	$3.39
—— Dividends	$1.62	$1.69	$1.72	$1.76	$1.80

If you invest $10,000 in AT&T in 2014, you can expect an annual dividend payment of $525. In 2019, the annual dividend payment will grow to $670. In 2034 the annual dividend payment will grow to $1,400.

From the chart above, earnings are erratic from year to year. This is fairly normal for a telecom company since they have large non-cash charges in some years. For example, depreciation on equipment may be accelerated, lowering earnings during the years where depreciation is high.

Chapter 22

Verizon Communications, Inc.

Verizon Communications Inc. (Ticker: VZ) is provider of communications, information and entertainment products to consumers, businesses and governmental agencies. It operates in two business segments: Verizon Wireless and Wireline. Verizon recently acquired EdgeCast Networks, Inc.

Verizon is known for two major services: Wireless & FiOS. Verizon Wireless is the largest carrier of mobile phone subscriptions with about 95 million subscribers. This accounts for 35 percent of the total U.S. market share. Verizon's FiOS television has over 5 million subscribers. Their main growth in sales will come from FiOS television subscriptions. They have a wide-open runway to grow FiOS subscriptions.

Verizon generates over $120 billion in revenue, with over $11 billion of that dropping to net income. Net income will fluctuate from year to year but will trend upward over many years. The revenue may seem very high, thus being hard to grow. Since the company has a small footprint in certain segments, it has room to grow revenues in these segments.

Like AT&T, Verizon operates in a highly competitive price driven environment. Verizon has to put a lot of money in acquiring new customers. It generates tons of cash from the wireless segment, so it can finance its growth in FiOS with the cash from wireless subscriptions.

Verizon Communications, Inc.

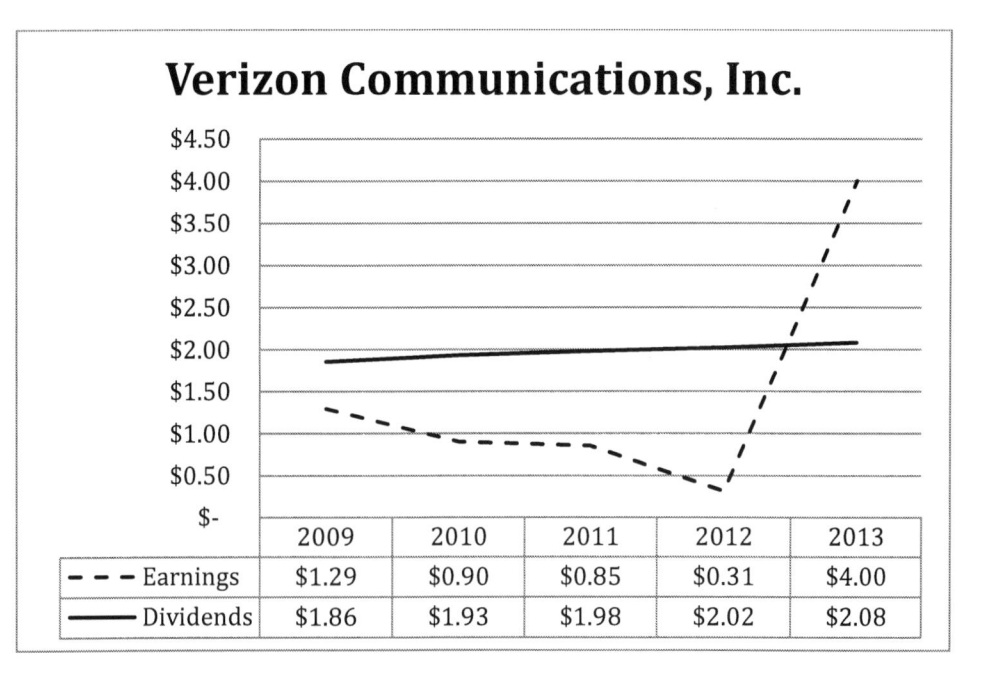

	2009	2010	2011	2012	2013
Earnings	$1.29	$0.90	$0.85	$0.31	$4.00
Dividends	$1.86	$1.93	$1.98	$2.02	$2.08

Verizon has a relatively high current dividend yield, at 4.5 percent. Its 5-year dividend growth rate is only 2.8 percent. This dividend growth rate should go to about 5 percent as Verizon grows its FiOS business. If you invest $10,000 in Verizon in 2014, you can expect an annual dividend payment of $450. In 2019, the annual dividend payment will grow to $570. In 2034 the annual dividend payment will grow to $1,200.

Chapter 23

Taxes

If you want to reach million dollar portfolio status, you have to avoid current taxes as much as possible. Tax avoidance is perfectly legal. In fact, in 1934 an American judge ruled: *'Anyone may arrange his affairs so that his taxes shall be as low as possible; he is not bound to choose that pattern which best pays the Treasury. There is not even a patriotic duty to increase one's taxes. Nobody owes any public duty to pay more than the law demands.'* You must shelter as much of your income from current taxes as possible in order to build your portfolio quickly. Fortunately, the tax system in the United States is full of deductions (incentives) for certain types of actions (behaviors).

If Uncle Sam wants you to do a certain thing (i.e. have a child, buy a home, cash in your clunker, etc.), he will offer you some sort of incentive to do so. The government wants citizens to save in designated retirement accounts, so you'll get a deduction off your income tax liability if you put money into a retirement account. The government wants its citizens to buy homes and thus offers a mortgage interest rate tax deduction. In addition to these normal deductions, you'll need to use strategic methods to get the most out of your current income.

Employees

Employees can reduce their tax liability using a few tax-favored savings plans and other options. The most notable tax shelter for employees is the 401(k) or 403(b) plan. This plan allows employees to defer up to $17,500 of income each year (as of 2014). This is quite generous given the median household income is just over $52,000. With this plan alone, the median household is able to defer 33 percent of its income. The problem with this is that most households that make $52,000 are unable to afford that type of savings rate, even before taxes. The single most powerful part of the 401(k)/403(b) plan is the company match. Most companies are now matching at least 50 percent of contributions up to 5 percent of the employee's annual income. Some companies are even matching dollar for dollar up to 6 percent of an employee's income. This is phenomenal since it's a totally voluntary program. Employers aren't required by law to offer a tax-deferred savings plan, and if they do, they don't have to match what the employee contributes.

The dividend growth investor should contribute at least the same amount the employer will match into their 401(k) or 403(b) plan. After all, it's free money, and a great return on your initial investment. A dollar for dollar match on five percent of your income could equal an extra $5,000 per year depending on your household income.

The biggest downfall to employer sponsored retirement plans is their investment options. Most plans offer a wide range of mutual funds, including target date funds, and sometimes even index funds. You may even find an option like the T. Rowe Price Dividend Growth Fund. The best option is most likely the one with the smallest expense ratio. Some of the institutional class index funds have expense ratios lower than a tenth of one percent. This is incredible considering some of the mutual fund options have expense ratios of over one percent. A great investment option is an index fund that tracks the S&P 500 index. This option will usually have a very low expense ratio, and it's relatively safe to put 100 percent of your contributions into it.

It's acceptable to not be in dividend stocks through your 401(k), but it's likely that in the future, you'll be able to trade individual stocks through your employer sponsored plan. Fidelity has a special plan they call BrokerageLink that connects investors to hundreds of fund options, but there's still no access to individual stocks. If employees demand more options in the future, plan administrators will have no choice but to add more investment choices, including individual stocks.

If you want to be invested in dividend growth ETFs or index funds, here are some options: Vanguard High Dividend Yield Index Fund (VYM), SPDR S&P Dividend ETF (SDY), WisdomTree LargeCap Dividend Fund (DLN), Vanguard Dividend Appreciation ETF (VIG), Schwab U.S. Dividend Equity ETF (SCHD), Vanguard Equity Income Fund (VEIPX), and T. Rowe Price Dividend Growth Fund (PRDGX).

Every time you change jobs, you can roll your retirement plan over into a self-directed individual retirement plan (an IRA). Never leave your old employer's retirement plan in place. Once you roll it into your own IRA, you'll be able to trade individual stocks and purchase companies listed in this book.

Self-Employed

Self-employed persons have three great options for tax-deferred retirement plans. The first option is the Simplified Employee Pension (SEP). This plan allows you to contribute as much as 25 percent of you net earnings up to $52,000 total (as of 2014). The power of this plan is incredible as long as your self-employed net earnings are high enough to contribute a substantial amount. It's easy to open a SEP. Search for "Form 5305-SEP" on Google, fill it out, and file it in your records. Then, go to an investment institution and open a SEP account. Fidelity's SEP plan is very popular with self-employed individuals. The requirements for opening a SEP are: you must be a sole propprietor, a business owner, in a partnership, or earn self-employment income by providing your services.

Another option for the self-employed individual is a 401(k) plan. Many people think that 401(k) plans are for employees only, but this is not the case. These plans are sometimes called "solo-401(k)", "individual 401(k)", or "uni-401(k)". For self-employed persons, the 401(k) plan is even more powerful. Not only can you contribute up to $17,500, but also an additional 25 percent of your net earnings up to $52,000 (not including contributions for yourself).

The last option is the SIMPLE IRA plan. This plan allows self-employed individuals to put all of their net earnings up to $12,000 tax-deferred and either a 2 percent fixed or 3 percent matching contribution. This plan is especially great for normal employees who also earn a modest consulting income. If you fit into this category, you could defer most, if not all, of your consulting income.

An entrepreneur with high net earnings in the range of $300,000 plus could defer a significant portion of his income. If this entrepreneur lived in a high tax area like New York City, he could avoid ever paying state and local income tax on almost half of his income by taking advantage of the above plans. After working for years in the high tax area, the entreprenuer, who squirreled away tax-deferrred money could then move to an income-tax-free state like Florida. No wonder there are so many retirees in Florida; it makes perfect sense! This shows the power of incentives in our lives. Government incentives can make citizens of one state flee to another state in retirement, all of which is perfectly legal.

Most plans for self-employed persons allow them to invest in individual stocks. This allows them to pick the best stocks for their overall dividend portfolio. Self-employment seems like such a great option. Not only can you make your own hours and have no official boss (except customers), your investment options are so much better than an employee's option. If you're not self-employed, this is a powerful motive to consider starting a small side business like consulting.

Investor

Earning a living as an investor has a very broad meaning. You could be an heir to a great ketchup fortune like Theresa Heinz-Kerry. You could also be an early retiree who has fought hard his whole life to build an income-generating portfolio. Either way, you have many advantages that the modern day working proletariat does not. For example, if you invest your ketchup money in municipal bonds like the aforementioned heiress, you will not pay a dime in federal income taxes and may escape a large portion of state income taxes. "That's not fair," you may say, but *c'est la vie*. If you've saved your whole life and your income derives from dividends, you'll pay 15 percent in federal income tax. If you have more than $400,000 in taxable income – and couples with more than $450,000 – you're taxed at 20 percent. If you're in one of the two lowest tax brackets, your dividends are not taxed at all! Dividends are taxed very favorably.

One reason for the low dividend tax rate is because they're already taxed at the corporate level. Dividends are paid out of a company's net income after tax. Most corporations' tax rates fall above 30 percent, so dividends are already coming from fairly highly taxed net income. There is no reason that this would change in the foreseeable future.

Chapter 24

Inflation

"Inflation is the one form of taxation that can be imposed without legislation." ~Milton Freidman

As I write this (beginning of 2014), the Federal Reserve is buying about $65 billion in securities each and every month. This is a slight improvement over the $85 billion they were buying during the entirety of 2013. One of the reasons the Fed is doing this is to counteract the deflationary effects brought on by the Great Recession of 2008-2009. As if lower prices are necessarily a bad thing, the Fed, in all its market-omniscience, said no to deflation. Ben Bernanke, being a scholar of the Great Depression, decided not to let the deflationary debt spiral happen on his watch. The merits of the initial bailout and stimulus by the government are not a topic of this book. It is well known that America is no longer a laissez-faire Capitalistic market system, but rather a government-managed Capitalistic market system.

Lower prices are the natural reaction during the downside of the business cycle. Indeed, deflation is the cure for recession. Low prices are a market reaction to clear out stock. One could argue that the Great Recession was no normal business cycle and they would be correct. It's insignificant for our discussion here though since we need not look at the noise (arguments over Fed decisions) but adjust for the signal (inflation). Since the Fed will do anything to avoid deflation – of any sort it seems – we can conclude that inflation will occur eventually. That inflation is a historical fact, and always occurs with fiat currencies, is objective. There is no argument that inflation is with us today, but the question is twofold. What is the real inflation rate? And, what will the inflation rate be in the future?

Currently, the inflation rate is at about 2 percent. Not bad you might say: inflation is so low, so why not keep printing money? The Federal Reserve in all their devious ways devised a scheme to mute the expected inflation rate. After implementing Quantitative Easing Two (QE2), the Fed instituted a policy decision called Operation Twist. Operation Twist is a bond market manipulation technique where the aim is to decrease long-term bond rates while increasing short-term bond rates. The Fed does this by selling the short-term bonds it has on its balance sheet and aggressively buying long-term bonds. The buying of the long-term bonds serves to push down bond yields, thus curbing the expected inflation rate for the future. The expected inflation rate is of utmost importance to investors.

Investing in an Inflationary Environment

As a dividend growth investor, it's important to pick stocks that grow at a minimum of twice the rate of current inflation. If inflation is running at 2 percent, annual growth in dividends should be at least 4 percent. A higher required growth percentage would eliminate some stocks with a very high current yield. For example, Kinder Morgan Partners, L.P. has a current dividend yield of 7.5 percent, but their dividend growth rate is 5 percent. This is perfectly acceptable because we value the high current yield, thus allowing for a lower growth rate. Notice here that the dividend growth rate is still 5 percent, not below the required rate of 4 percent.

Stocks with no growth in dividends from year to year should be avoided. No growth in dividends could signal that the company is not growing earnings or the dividend payout ratio is too high. When you account for economic inflation, companies that don't grow their dividends actually have a falling real dividend. If a company has a $1 dividend per year for five years in a row, the value of the dividend in the fifth year is less than in the first year. Inflation has slowly eroded the purchasing power of the $1 dividend. It may now only buy you $0.80 of goods or services. It may not seem like a lot at first, but it starts to add up if your portfolio generates $10,000 in dividends every year.

Companies that can pass inflation costs onto consumers will be more successful in times of high inflation. McDonald's is a good example of a company that can pass on a rise in costs. If overall inflation rises to 5 percent annually, McDonald's can quickly and easily raise prices to match inflation. As long as consumers can keep their incomes at or above the rate of inflation, McDonald's will not be affected. Companies that sell products that are used immediately or almost immediately (non-durables) to consumers are protected from inflation.

Companies that hold long-term contracts or hold long-term bonds will not fair well during times of high inflation. Many banks and insurance companies hold long-term assets like long-term bonds and mortgage-backed securities. For example, AFLAC, Inc. (Ticker: AFL) holds many long-term bonds. When inflation rises, these bonds will become worth less to an investor. Why would an investor want a 3 percent coupon 30-year bond when he can buy a 5 percent 30-year bond? He wouldn't buy the 3 percent coupon 30-year bond unless he could buy it at less than face value. The price of AFLAC's bond holdings will have to go down when prevailing interest rates rise. This is why it is so difficult to value insurance companies and banks. They're full of assets that are interest rate sensitive.

The stocks recommended in this book will outperform many other companies during times of high inflation. REITs and MLPs will be put under pressure but will perform fine. Companies that sell consumer non-durable goods will outperform all other companies during times of high inflation.

Chapter 25

Reaching a Million

"Luck is the residue of design."

~Branch Rickey

Branch Rickey was the manager of the Brooklyn Dodgers, who against popular opinion at the time, signed the first black player, Jackie Robinson. He often said that, "luck is the residue of design" – meaning that those who plan are those who are the lucky ones.

Many people attribute success to random luck, family name, or lack of ethics. This couldn't be further from the truth. Success or "luck" is the byproduct of hard work and, most importantly, a plan. It's true that some people are born into wealth and/or a family name that gives them a leg up in society. Others are born into a single-parent household with few resources, leaving them desperately struggling at the margins of society. The vast majority of Americans, however, fall somewhere in the middle.

For the vast majority of Americans in the middle, having a plan is a key ingredient for future financial success. Those who live paycheck-to-paycheck sometimes make excuses so that they don't have to face their financial reality. They may say that there are just too many bills to pay each month to save money. They may also blame it on their boss for not giving them that big raise or promotion. This type of thought process can be self-destructive, never allowing any ownership for their lot in life.

This kind of behavior can be found in the group that called themselves the "99-percent" or the "Occupy Movement". This group of people believed that they could demand retribution for some perceived social and economic inequality that they faced. For example, a common perceived unfairness was the protesters' large amount of student loan debt. They believed that the government (read taxpayer) should forgive their tens of thousands of dollars in student loans. Where's the personal responsibility here? There is none, and that is a dangerous mindset to enter. When a person believes that the world owes them a break, they'll always be the victims of their life instead of the leaders.

One big idea that these 99-percenters should focus on is that if they want something, they'll have to work for it. Maybe they're upset because they believe they're working hard but not getting paid enough. Maybe they believe that the evil bankers have too much money. None of this really matters because the mentality that the 99-percenters hold is what makes them poor. The kind of person who is jealous of those who appear to have more material possession is poor in spirit.

People who take accountability and personal responsibility are far ahead when it comes to succeeding in life. If you're like this, you'll generally blame yourself for all of your failures. You'll understand that only you have the power to change your life's situation. You'll understand that life is not fair, and you may have to work harder than other people. You will learn the importance of having a plan.

Achieving a million dollar portfolio is not a quick and easy feat. You'll have to increase you income, lower your expenses, and invest the balance wisely. You'll have to put a plan down on paper, use tools, and gain knowledge. The first thing you'll have to do is figure out your monthly net income (or loss) in a business-like manner.

How Much Do You Net?

The fastest way to increase your investable income is to increase the difference between your income and your expenses. Imagine that your household is a business. You make money as an employee or self-employed person. This is your gross revenue (earned income). Then, you have your operating expenses, other income (passive), other expenses (tax, new roof, etc.), and finally your total net income.

	Revenues		
	Employee Revenue	_____	
	Self-Employed Revenue	_____	
	Cost of Self-Employed Revenue	-	
A	Gross Profit / (Loss)		_____
	Operating Expenses		
	Mortgage	_____	+
	Utilities	_____	+
	Food	_____	+
	Vehicle	_____	+
	Administrative	_____	
B	Total Operating Expenses		_____
C	Income From Operations (A-B)		_____
	Other Income		
	Dividend Income	_____	
	Interest Income	_____	
D	Total Other Income		_____
E	Income From Operations plus Other Income (C+D)		_____
	Other Expenses		
	One-time capital expenditure	_____	+
	Miscellaneous	_____	+
	Tax Expense	_____	+
F	Total Other Expenses		_____
G	**Net Income / (loss) (E-F)**		_____

Use monthly data to fill out this table (also available on www.thefinanceshow.com in Excel format), then you'll be able to compute your monthly net income / (loss) amount on line "G". Your goal is to have the highest net income possible so that you can invest this amount into dividend-paying stocks, or other investments. Find out your net income percentage by dividing net income by line "A" Gross Profit. A recommended percentage goal is to have at least 25 percent "drop" to net income. If you can increase your income and decrease your expense to achieve this percentage, you'll be able to achieve million-dollar portfolio status much more quickly.

Increasing Your Income

Increasing your income may seem impossible at times, but if you continue to pursue consulting work or other self-employed income, you will increase your income in due time. Many people try something new; realize it doesn't provide enough income, and then move on to the next thing. You have to stick with something for at least six months before you know if it's a winner or not.

Some ventures will flame out quickly and some will take some time before you know they're losers. If you start a website or podcast, it may take at least six months to catch on. Don't give up after the first two posts or episodes. Starting to work freelance jobs on www.elance.com can seem daunting at first, but after a while, people will know you're good and hire you for better pay.

Brainstorm to see how many different ways you can increase your income. This may seem trite, but nothing gets done until you put it on paper. Write a list of twenty ways to double your salary over the next year. This is an ambitious goal, but this will allow you to see what you'll need to do in order to garnish a higher income. It could be something like getting a degree, a license, or networking. Maybe it's starting a business or writing the next great American novel. Items that are on this list have one thing in common: all of them will make you a more marketable person.

Abundance Over Scarcity

Saving money is generally a virtue, but focusing all of your efforts on pinching every penny can breed an environment of scarcity. This type of environment can be unpleasant for you and everyone around you. Having the scarcity mentality means that you're not really living life like you should be. You're too busy worried about the cost of daily living. This type of mentality will force you to stay indoors, not drive your car, turn the heater down in the winter time, and eat rice and beans every day. It's no fun. People who succumb to this mentality will not be able to achieve their potential (whatever their creative endeavors may be), because their mind is too busy with scrimping and saving. If this person would, instead, think as if nothing were scarce, they would be able to unleash more cerebral power, which would fill their lives with abundance.

    That's why it's not as important to focus on saving, as much as it is to focus on earning more money and investing it wisely. Saving money and being a good steward of money is still important though. I'm not saying don't keep a budget and don't worry about how you're spending your money, quite the opposite. You should try to save money effectively, not worrying about the small behavioral expenditures. You should instead focus on the large, structural expenses like homes and vehicles.

    There are some behavioral expenses that make people happy on a daily basis and aren't significant in the long run. Items like: lattes, lunches out, baked goods, all make people happy. Sure, you could cut these items out of your life and save one thousand or so dollars a year, but then you'd be cutting out some of the happiness in your life. Why would anyone want to trade-in their happiness for the accumulation of a thousand dollars a year? I would rather work a couple of weekends and be able to buy coffee out every day of the year, wouldn't you? It makes more sense to make big changes to your expenses. These are called structural changes.

    Making structural changes to your expenses is a more effective way to spend fewer dollars, and it can be easier than giving up your daily latte. Changes like refinancing your home, buying a five-year-old car instead of a brand new one, or buying a smaller home instead of a McMansion, are all structural changes. These are more permanent changes, and can same hundreds, sometimes thousands every month. Not only will you save more money with these types of changes, you're also likely to be just as happy without a McMansion or new car.

Economists have shown that there is a diminishing return for each additional unit of utility. Utility, in the case of a structural change, would be the happiness derived from a new car. With each turn of the new car's ignition, the owner is a little less satisfied with their purchase. It's not that the owner doesn't like the car. It's that the car quickly becomes just another tool for the owner. Their initial happiness fades and they fall back to a happiness-equilibrium.

Boosting Your Portfolio

Building a portfolio can be a daunting task if you're starting at zero or a negative amount. It can be very difficult for someone in his or her early twenties, making a modest income, to think about saving money every month. They may not be able to pay all their bills or may be deep in student loan debt. If you find yourself in a situation where you need to jumpstart your portfolio, you need to take drastic actions much like Sarah did in Chapter 1. Depending on your stage in life, here's a list of things you can do to boost your portfolio:

- Join the military
- Take on a roommate
- Get a second job
- Take on consulting work
- Start a business
- Buy a multi-unit property; live in one and rent the others
- Get a higher degree
- Ask for a raise
- Get licensed in your field
- Sell on eBay or Amazon

- Refinance your home
- Invent a product
- Provide a service

All of the items on this list have the potential to allow people to boost their portfolio. Some of these items are quite drastic. For example, I wouldn't recommend joining the military unless you really want to serve the country in that way. Anything done for the sole purpose of gaining financial resources is likely to be a mistake. If you're just starting out in life, pick something from this list that you actually want to do. If you absolutely hate sitting in a classroom, why would you want to go back and get your master's degree? Aside from the onerous cost of obtaining the degree, you'll be miserable for at least a year.

If you think you're going to be able to build a sizable portfolio by sitting in your cube all day, you've been lied to. Some high-income jobs do exist, but remember that being an employee is the hardest way to build wealth. Employees have to rely on their company or boss to increase their pay. Their pay is loosely linked to merit, with modest raises given usually once per year. One exception to this is sales. Companies will usually pay their sales people based on the revenue generated by the sales person. If you're in sales, it may be easier to attain a high income, even at a young age.

Business and Investing

In order to achieve a million dollar portfolio, you'll have to work on being in business for yourself and honing your investing skills. Being in business for yourself doesn't necessarily mean that you should start a business. Starting a business might not be the right choice, especially if you have to give up everything just to open the business. Being in business for yourself is defined as deriving an income (a scalable income if possible) from a product that you create or a service that you render.

Scalable businesses allow the businessperson to leverage their effort and talent. It's difficult to build wealth quickly working for a company that pays by the hour or a set salary. It's also a quick way to burnout. Hourly workers who try to simply work more hours to get ahead soon find out that more effort will lead to burnout and frustration. With a scalable business, the businessperson puts a lot of hard work in during the initial build-out phase. Then, the product is launched and scaled to a customer base. Some products will draw little attention and fail, while others will be a hit and sell heavy volume.

Planning for A Million

Investing is an iterative process that should be planned, implemented, and evaluated. The first step in the planning phase is to figure out what should be gained from investing. In this book, the focus is on achieving a million dollar portfolio so that the investor can live off of the dividend income the portfolio generates. To achieve this goal, the investor needs to take multiple steps. Knowing the numbers that it takes to achieve the final goal empowers the investor. Instead of guessing or hoping about their goals, the investor can take solace in the fact that their plan is on target.

The formula used to calculate a future portfolio value is straightforward; here are the inputs:

- Initial Portfolio Balance
- Dividend Payment
- Appreciation
- Additional Investments

With these four inputs, you can calculate when you'll reach your goal of a one million dollar portfolio. You'll also be able to figure out how much in dividends you'll make each year and estimate how much in stock price appreciation (unrealized gains) you'll make each year. For the following chart, assume that you start with a portfolio of $100,000, receive 5 percent in dividend payments, receive 8 percent in stock appreciation, and add an additional $24,000 to your portfolio each year. All dividends are reinvested at current rates

Year	Portfolio Balance	Dividend Payment	Appreciation	Investments
1	$ 100,000	$ 5,000	$ 8,000	$ 24,000
2	$ 137,000	$ 6,850	$ 10,960	$ 24,000
3	$ 178,810	$ 8,941	$ 14,305	$ 24,000
4	$ 226,055	$ 11,303	$ 18,084	$ 24,000
5	$ 279,442	$ 13,972	$ 22,355	$ 24,000
6	$ 339,770	$ 16,989	$ 27,182	$ 24,000
7	$ 407,940	$ 20,397	$ 32,635	$ 24,000
8	$ 484,972	$ 24,249	$ 38,798	$ 24,000
9	$ 572,019	$ 28,601	$ 45,761	$ 24,000
10	$ 670,381	$ 33,519	$ 53,630	$ 24,000
11	$ 781,531	$ 39,077	$ 62,522	$ 24,000
12	$ 907,130	$ 45,356	$ 72,570	$ 24,000
13	$ 1,049,057	$ 52,453	$ 83,925	$ 24,000
14	$ 1,209,434	$ 60,472	$ 96,755	$ 24,000
15	$ 1,390,660	$ 69,533	$ 111,253	$ 24,000
16	$ 1,595,446	$ 79,772	$ 127,636	$ 24,000
17	$ 1,826,854	$ 91,343	$ 146,148	$ 24,000
18	$ 2,088,345	$ 104,417	$ 167,068	$ 24,000
19	$ 2,383,830	$ 119,192	$ 190,706	$ 24,000
20	$ 2,717,728	$ 135,886	$ 217,418	$ 24,000
21	$ 3,095,033	$ 154,752	$ 247,603	$ 24,000
22	$ 3,521,387	$ 176,069	$ 281,711	$ 24,000
23	$ 4,003,167	$ 200,158	$ 320,253	$ 24,000
24	$ 4,547,579	$ 227,379	$ 363,806	$ 24,000
25	$ 5,162,764	$ 258,138	$ 413,021	$ 24,000

With these inputs, you can see from the chart that you'll become a millionaire by your thirteenth year of the plan. This is very fast and was made possible by the large initial investment and the large additions to the portfolio. During the thirteenth year, the annual dividend payment is over $52,000. Some, if not all, of these dividends may be shielded from tax depending on which vehicle they're invested in. If all of the dividends were held in a taxable account, the tax due would still only be approximately

$7,800, leaving the investor $44,200 in net income. It's important to remember that the value of future dollars is less due to inflation. How much less is up for debate, but inflation will eventually pick up in the United States, and it could pick up rapidly.

Even if you don't make a contribution after your initial deposit, you can still expect to achieve a million dollar portfolio by your twentieth year. Notice also that during the twentieth year, you're annual dividend payment amount is close to $51,000. This is quite extraordinary, especially since no additional investments were made each year.

Year	Portfolio Balance	Dividend Payment	Appreciation	Investments
1	$ 100,000	$ 5,000	$ 8,000	$ -
2	$ 113,000	$ 5,650	$ 9,040	$ -
3	$ 127,690	$ 6,385	$ 10,215	$ -
4	$ 144,290	$ 7,214	$ 11,543	$ -
5	$ 163,047	$ 8,152	$ 13,044	$ -
6	$ 184,244	$ 9,212	$ 14,739	$ -
7	$ 208,195	$ 10,410	$ 16,656	$ -
8	$ 235,261	$ 11,763	$ 18,821	$ -
9	$ 265,844	$ 13,292	$ 21,268	$ -
10	$ 300,404	$ 15,020	$ 24,032	$ -
11	$ 339,457	$ 16,973	$ 27,157	$ -
12	$ 383,586	$ 19,179	$ 30,687	$ -
13	$ 433,452	$ 21,673	$ 34,676	$ -
14	$ 489,801	$ 24,490	$ 39,184	$ -
15	$ 553,475	$ 27,674	$ 44,278	$ -
16	$ 625,427	$ 31,271	$ 50,034	$ -
17	$ 706,733	$ 35,337	$ 56,539	$ -
18	$ 798,608	$ 39,930	$ 63,889	$ -
19	$ 902,427	$ 45,121	$ 72,194	$ -
20	$ 1,019,742	$ 50,987	$ 81,579	$ -
21	$ 1,152,309	$ 57,615	$ 92,185	$ -
22	$ 1,302,109	$ 65,105	$ 104,169	$ -
23	$ 1,471,383	$ 73,569	$ 117,711	$ -
24	$ 1,662,663	$ 83,133	$ 133,013	$ -
25	$ 1,878,809	$ 93,940	$ 150,305	$ -

This chart includes numbers that may seem out of reach to a small time investor. If you have a very small income and limited funds to invest, you need to increase your income before you focus on investing. The biggest wealth-building tool is a high income, whether you're an employee, self-employed, or a small business person.

Dividend Performance Indicator

When picking stocks to hold for the long-term, the dividend growth investor looks for two main variables: dividend yield and dividend growth rate. Of course, there are many other things to look for including: dividend payment history, earnings trend, valuation ratios, and others. The Dividend Performance Indicator (DPI – see Appendix A) focuses on the two main components. It is a measure that multiplies the dividend yield and the dividend growth rate. For example, a stock that yields 5 percent and has a dividend growth rate of 10 percent has a dividend performance indicator of 50. The DPI is a very quick and easy measure that allows the dividend growth investor to see if a stock passes an initial screen. Based on future-payment analysis, no stocks that have a DPI of less than 30 should be purchased for a dividend growth portfolio. A DPI of less than 30 either indicates that the stock has a very low yield or a very low rate of dividend growth.

Taking Advantage of Mr. Market

Planning on achieving a million dollar portfolio is made easier by the whims of Mr. Market. Some investors think that wild swings in the stock market are a good reason to stay in cash. This is the wrong way to approach investing. In the very long run, the stock market is much smoother. An investor who checks his account every day is listening to the noise in his portfolio, instead of listening for buy and sell signals. No one knows what a stock will do in one trading day. Prices are driven by greed, fear, supercomputers, hedge funds, and many headline driven retail investors. If you can block out all of the noise, instead focusing on fundamental signals, you can make money in the market. When a stock price is discounted because some talking head went on CNBC to disparage it, you can buy the stock knowing that the underlying business is sound. One of the best times to buy a good company is when other people are selling it and many people are telling you not to buy it.

When the British Petroleum (BP) Oil spill happened in April 2010, the company's stock price took a major hit. The stock went from $57 per share down to $27 per share with two months. At the bottom, very few market participants wanted to own BP's shares. If you had taken advantage of this hysteria and purchased BP shares at $27, you would have been reward handsomely. The stock finished 2010 at $47 per share, a 74 percent gain. Not only would you have gained the 74 percent in price appreciation, you would have also had a stock that paid a large dividend. BP did skip a few dividend payments, but this was just a temporary issue. The noise was very loud; many saying that BP would go bankrupt. This scared investors greatly, thus allowing calm investors to come in and buy BP's stock. Anyone with third grade math skills could see that BP would not go bankrupt from the oil spill. To this company, $42.2 (estimated civil and criminal fines from 2010 - 2014) billion is not the end of the business but rather a large bump in the road. [It should be noted that BP was not entirely at fault for the spill. The *Deepwater Horizon* rig was built by Hyundai, owned by Transocean, and chartered by BP and other partners, including Halliburton.]

Conclusion

In order to achieve a million-dollar dividend portfolio, the investor needs to be disciplined, patient, and educated. The stocks in this book will give any dividend investor the edge needed to build a solid portfolio. Investors need to put capital to work in the right types of accounts, whether they are tax-deferred or taxable. A relatively high income is needed in order to build up capital quickly in the initial years. Once the investor's portfolio reaches six-figures, compounding works its magic. Many investors can reach a million-dollar portfolio within 20 years.

If you're just starting your dividend portfolio, it's good to start with big blue-chip companies that have a long track record of rewarding shareholders. Initial stock purchases should include companies like Phillip Morris International (Ticker: PM) and Coca-Cola (Ticker: KO). After you're comfortable with normal equities, it's time to branch out to REITs and MLPs (make sure you know all about taxes before buying these types of assets).

At first, it may be hard to have a diversified portfolio. You should strive to hold at least 12 stocks in your portfolio, even if you only have $1,000 to invest in each stock in the beginning. Holding more than 20 different stocks will make keeping track of your companies much more difficult, but you will not gain much more in marginal diversification. Invest in between 12 and 20 stocks.

Holding stocks in different sectors is important to staying diversified. You wouldn't want every stock in your portfolio to be in the oil and gas industry. If oil prices fall, every one of your stocks would likely fall. Don't buy a stock if you're not willing to hold it for 10 years.

Your dividend payments will grow each and every year. It's difficult to imagine in the beginning years, but you'll be able to live off of your dividends in the future. Stick with dividend growth stocks and you'll be on your way to a million-dollar portfolio.

Acknowledgments

My first-line editor and friend, Manon Loiseau, did a wonderful job scouring a very rough draft making it comprehensible and grammatically correct. I can't thank you enough for your time on this book.

I am also grateful to my beta-reader and executive editor, Hank Jordan, for his leadership on making this into a book. Your years of experience with technical editing show throughout the pages of this book. Thank you.

Appendix A: Dividend Performance Indicator Chart

Current Dividend Yield

Dividend Growth Rate	3.0	3.1	3.2	3.3	3.4	3.5	3.6	3.7	3.8	3.9	4.0	4.1	4.2	4.3	4.4	4.5
5.0	15	16	16	17	17	18	18	19	19	20	20	21	21	22	22	23
5.5	17	17	18	18	19	19	20	20	21	21	22	23	23	24	24	25
6.0	18	19	19	20	20	21	22	22	23	23	24	25	25	26	26	27
6.5	20	20	21	21	22	23	23	24	25	25	26	27	27	28	29	29
7.0	21	22	22	23	24	25	25	26	27	27	28	29	29	30	31	32
7.5	23	23	24	25	26	26	27	28	29	29	30	31	32	32	33	34
8.0	24	25	26	26	27	28	29	30	30	31	32	33	34	34	35	36
8.5	26	26	27	28	29	30	31	31	32	33	34	35	36	37	37	38
9.0	27	28	29	30	31	32	32	33	34	35	36	37	38	39	40	41
9.5	29	29	30	31	32	33	34	35	36	37	38	39	40	41	42	43
10.0	30	31	32	33	34	35	36	37	38	39	40	41	42	43	44	45
10.5	32	33	34	35	36	37	38	39	40	41	42	43	44	45	46	47
11.0	33	34	35	36	37	39	40	41	42	43	44	45	46	47	48	50
11.5	35	36	37	38	39	40	41	43	44	45	46	47	48	49	51	52
12.0	36	37	38	40	41	42	43	44	46	47	48	49	50	52	53	54

http://tinyurl.com/dividendperformanceindicator

Appendix B: Budget

	Revenues		
	Employee Revenue		
	Self-Employed Revenue		
	Cost of Self-Employed Revenue		-
A	Gross Profit / (Loss)		
	Operating Expenses		
	Mortgage		+
	Utilities		+
	Food		+
	Vehicle		+
	Administrative		
B	Total Operating Expenses		
C	Income From Operations (A-B)		
	Other Income		
	Dividend Income		
	Interest Income		
D	Total Other Income		
E	Income From Operations plus Other Income (C+D)		
	Other Expenses		
	One-time capital expenditure		+
	Miscellaneous		+
	Tax Expense		+
F	Total Other Expenses		
G	**Net Income / (loss) (E-F)**		

http://tinyurl.com/dividendmillionairebudget

References

Phillip Morris International, Inc. (2013). *Annual report 2013*. Retrieved from http://investors.pmi.com/phoenix.zhtml?c=146476&p=irol-reportsannual

Realty Income (2013). *Annual report 2013*, Retrieved from http://www.realtyincome.com/investing/2014-annual-docs.shtml

The Southern Company (2012). *Annual report 2012*, Retrieved from http://investor.southerncompany.com/annuals.cfm

McDonald's Corp (2012). *Annual report 2012*, Retrieved from http://www.aboutmcdonalds.com/mcd/investors/annual_reports.html

Kraft Foods (2013). *Annual report 2013*, Retrieved from http://ir.kraftfoodsgroup.com/annuals.cfm

ConAgra Foods Corp (2013). *Annual report 2013*, Retrieved from http://www.conagrafoods.com/investor-relations/financial-reports/annual-reports

The Coca-Cola Corp (2013). *Annual report 2013*, Retrieved from http://www.coca-colacompany.com/investors/annual-other-reports

Pepsico, Inc. (2013). *Annual report 2013*, Retrieved from http://www.pepsico.com/Investors/Annual-Reports-and-Proxy-Information

Potash Corp. of Saskatchewan (2013). *Annual report 2013*, Retrieved from http://www.potashcorp.com/investors/financial_reporting/annual/

ConocoPhillips (2013). *Annual report 2013*, Retrieved from http://www.conocophillips.com/investor-relations/company-reports/Pages/default.aspx

Altria Group, Inc. (2013). *Annual report 2013*, Retrieved from http://investor.altria.com/phoenix.zhtml?c=80855&p=irol-reportsannual

Kinder Morgan Partners, L.P. (2013). *Annual report 2013*, Retrieved from http://www.kindermorgan.com/investor/kmp_annual_reports.cfm

Enterprise Products Partners, L.P. (2013). *Annual report 2013*, Retrieved from http://www.annualreports.com/Company/1359

Kinder Morgan, Inc. (2013). *Annual report 2013*, Retrieved from http://www.kindermorgan.com/investor/kmp_annual_reports.cfm

Kimberly-Clark Corp. (2013). *Annual report 2012*, Retrieved from https://www.kimberly-clark.com/investors/financial_information/annualreports.aspx?print=true

Procter & Gamble (2013). *Annual report 2013*, Retrieved from http://www.pginvestor.com/GenPage.aspx?IID=4004124&GKP=1073748359

Johnson & Johnson (2013). *Annual report 2013*, Retrieved from http://www.investor.jnj.com/annual-reports.cfm

The Clorox Co (2013). *Annual report 2013*, Retrieved from http://www.thecloroxcompany.com/investors/financial-reporting/annual-reports/

AT&T (2013). *Annual report 2013*, Retrieved from http://www.att.com/gen/investor-relations?pid=9186

Verizon Communications, Inc. (2013). *Annual report 2013*, Retrieved from http://www.verizon.com/investor/quicklink.htm

Made in the USA
Lexington, KY
17 April 2015